how to avoid divorce

how to avoid divorce

LUCIANO L'ABATE and BESS L'ABATE

JOHN KNOX PRESS
ATLANTA

Library of Congress Cataloging in Publication Data

L'Abate, Luciano, 1928–
  How to avoid divorce.

    1. Marriage—United States. 2. Marriage counseling—United States. 3. Marriage counseling—United States—Directories. I. L'Abate, Bess, 1926– joint author. II. Title.
HQ734.L13   362.8'2   76–12389
ISBN 0-8042-1118-3

© John Knox Press 1977
Printed in the United States of America

contents

Introduction — 7

Section I Becoming Aware
    Chapter 1 Dreams About Marriage — 15
    Chapter 2 Checklist for Troubled Marriages — 22
    Chapter 3 More Checks — 39

Section II What Are the Possibilities?
    Chapter 4 How Do Marriages Become Troubled? — 49
    Chapter 5 Considering Changes — 56
    Chapter 6 Asking for Help — 69
    Chapter 7 Fighting Change: Arguments Against Help — 77
    Chapter 8 Avoiding Change: Shortcuts Won't Help! — 83
    Chapter 9 Religion and Change: Its Uses and Abuses — 88

Section III Doing Something Positive for a Change
    Chapter 10 Seeking Help in Groups — 95
    Chapter 11 Finding a Helper — 109
    Chapter 12 Seeking Private Helpers — 114
    Chapter 13 Getting Help — 121
    Chapter 14 Making Help Work: Getting Hold of Yourself — 126
    Chapter 15 The Tasks of Marriage Enhancement — 132
    Chapter 16 When Help Seems to Fail — 137

INTRODUCTION
is your marriage troubled?

"I'm not sure I want to go on with this marriage."
"If you don't like it, you know what you can do . . ."
"Do you mean that?"
"Of course I mean it! I don't like it any more than you do."
"I'll call a lawyer first thing in the morning."
"The sooner, the better for me, and take the kids with you."

. . .

"I'm sick and tired of your blaming me and finding fault . . . I won't take it any more."
"If you can't take it, get the hell out of here."
"It's fine with me . . ."

Confrontations like the two above are universal. Millions of couples who have confronted each other this way settle their unhappiness and troubled marriages by physical separation and/or legal divorce. Only after the final divorce decree is granted, however, do they discover that many issues relating to and stemming from the marriage are still present and unresolved, especially if there are children involved. While there is a physical separation and a legal divorce, the emotional ties have not been severed. The painful relationship still exists. Instead of these two extreme choices—a constantly painful marriage or no marriage—this book suggests that in between these extremes are many possibilities and choices available for those couples who want a better marriage and are not interested in divorce as the ultimate solution.

The choice between a lousy marriage and no marriage *can be* a *better* marriage. It may come as a shock to the reader to realize that marriages are not made in heaven. We need to work at them and invest in them if they are to succeed. However, most marriages do not get better all by themselves any more than our car can repair itself without the help of an expert mechanic. Most marriages, no matter how good and ideal, can stand an occasional overhaul so that they can run better. They need outside help like anything we want to improve in nature.

Very recently my wife and I saw a couple who had been married thirty-eight years, most of them unhappy. Nevertheless, they were still together and had no intention of breaking up in spite of many troubles. The husband was a retired president of a company he had founded. He had only a high school diploma ("If I want a Ph.D., I can hire one"). In addition to being a self-made business success, he was also a self-taught man. As his wife said: "There is nothing he can't fix." Despite all of these assets, neither he nor his wife had been willing to seek help for themselves. Now the husband had to face the fact that the most important relationship in his life—his marriage—could not be "fixed" all by itself. Only extreme pressure would force him to face the need to improve his marriage through external help.

Outside of our relationship to ourselves—what each of us feels, thinks, and says to oneself—marriage is the most important basic relationship one can have as an adult. This book is for all of us who are married or have been married, and have seen the healing as well as hurtful powers of marriage in ourselves, those we love, our parents, our brother and sisters, our friends and our neighbors.

This book is for couples who want to make their marriages better and not for those who want to keep their marriages as they are or who are ready to jump on to the other extreme, divorce.

We have become convinced that healthy, happy marriages usually include three important processes for personal fulfillment and growing that have not been sufficiently emphasized elsewhere. They are (a) marriage as self-confrontation, (b) marriage as reconciliation of differences, and (c) marriage as sharing of hurt feelings. The mounting divorce rate is due to the breakdown of one or more of these three basic functions. We may naturally prefer to avoid self-confrontation and choose to focus on the shortcomings of our mate to avoid looking at and into our own selves and behavior. Thus, we are unable to come to terms, consider, confront, negotiate, and integrate our differences, using them to make our marriages stronger and not weaker. Finally, we are unable to deal properly with our feelings of hurt and fear of being hurt by using these feelings to keep ourselves apart from each other rather than to use these feelings to come closer together.

Marriage is one of the most intense and explosive relationships in human lives. It can build or it can destroy. It can help or it can hinder. It can hurt or it can heal. Marriage can do or cannot do many things to us and for us. What it does to us is what we let it do. We are responsible for what our marriage is or is not. No one else is.

Society, religion, or other forces are often blamed for the collapse of our marriage. In this book we take a different approach. *How to Avoid Divorce* is for couples, any couples, who are striving, trying, and struggling to make a better marriage for themselves and for each other. While no book in and by itself can help every marriage, this book offers a personal and practical approach to making marriage more satisfying. It is what each of us will do with what is offered, however, that can make the basic difference.

It will be helpful to your marriage if both partners read this book. It will be less helpful if just one of you reads it and the other refuses to even consider and look at it. This book was written to help you deal with your marriage. It is not meant to help you with anybody else's marriage but your own. Consequently, read for your own pleasure and enjoyment and not anyone else's. If you do not find it helpful, keep looking for whatever will be useful for your own situation.

This book is not meant to help you deal with your parents' marriage or your children's marriages. As much as you may care for them and want them to be happy, the best way you can take care of them is through taking care of your own happiness and your own marriage. Put your energy where it counts, in your *marriage*. If you take care of yourself and your marriage, you will make it easier for them to take care of themselves and their marriages. Sometimes we interfere in the lives of others as a way of avoiding dealing with our own lives. The best way to help others is to help yourself. It is easy to help others; it is much more difficult to help oneself.

The most important question you may need to answer in the next few chapters is whether your marriage is in trouble or not. We will give some signs, cues, guidelines, and hints. None of the signs and cues we list may apply to you. However, if you do not feel happy about yourself and your marriage, that fact itself will tell you that your marriage is in trouble. Only you can judge whether you are happy or not. Do not let anyone tell you otherwise or sway you from your decision, since your feelings of unhappiness count more than what anybody else thinks about them. Your feelings are important, and if you have decided that you are unhappy, you have the right to be heard and you are entitled to do something about it.

What Is Unhappiness?

Happiness or unhappiness is a matter of feelings—how you feel. If you are feeling miserable, sad, grumpy, frigid, short-tempered, impatient, apathetic, or listless, you may be unhappy. If you are unhappy, your marriage is troubled. If you are happy, satisfied, enthusiastic, at peace with yourself and can accept things as they are, then your marriage very likely may not be troubled. On the other hand, you may feel happy, contented, and satisfied, but is your mate? You may need to check with your mate whether the way you feel is shared by him or her. If your feelings are not shared by your mate, then you may need to check on whether yours is a troubled marriage, and if it is troubled, how seriously troubled?

No one can feel how troubled your marriage is except you. No matter what others will tell you, you are the final judge on whether your marriage is troubled or not. We all know of people who are viewed as ideal couples by others. After all, they are successful, attractive, have a beautiful home and lovely children. But only they know what goes on among them behind the beautiful front.

What Unhappiness Entitles Us To:

Unhappiness entitles us to be heard.
Unhappiness entitles us to change.
Unhappiness entitles us to take responsibility for our unhappiness and not to put it on anyone else in our family.

Introduction

> *Unhappiness entitles us to work for changes in ourselves and in our marriage.*
>
> *Unhappiness entitles us to show how important we are.*
>
> *Unhappiness entitles us to work toward happiness. If we cannot work for happiness, then we must work for personal satisfaction, contentment, pride, and enjoyment. They are more visible and touchable goals than "happiness."*

Unhappiness does not entitle us to rob banks, get drunk, gamble, nag our loved ones to death, have temper tantrums, etc. We are not entitled to stay unhappy and make everybody else around us unhappy. We are not entitled to beat others over the head with it.

Who Needs a Painful Marriage?

We cannot tell marital partners how to live their lives. We feel very strongly that marital partners decide on what kind of marriage they will have. If they want a troubled marriage and they like it that way, they have the right to it. Unhappy marriages make many partners feel important. They can use the unhappiness in their marriage to complain, and they get attention and sympathy through their unhappiness. We know they need a troubled marriage when they continually talk about their unhappiness and *do nothing to change it!* Therefore, we are driven to conclude that many people need an unhappy marriage and in some cases get satisfaction, martyrdom, sympathy, attention, and other rewards from these marriages. It would be foolish for anybody to try to change marriages of this type. Both partners may have agreed, oftentimes openly and directly, that they get more through an unhappy marriage than through a happy one. Who are we to tell them otherwise? You will be surprised how many partners like their marriages the way they are: boring, meaningless, and in some ways self-destructive. It is our right to live our lives the way we want to and it cannot be taken away from us.

This book will not attempt to change the lives of those who are happy with what they have. It may be helpful to those who have a good marriage but may want a better one. It may be helpful for those who do not have a workable marriage and do not know how to achieve one. It may not be helpful to those with seriously troubled marriages.

People have the freedom to live their lives in self-defeating ways; they have the freedom not to change. If they do not want to change under any conditions, this book will not help them. Clearly this book is for those couples, those partners who want change for the better in their lives and in their marriages. *It will not help those who do not want change for the better.*

(Note: The authors use the construction (s)he when referring to characteristics which could belong to either husband *or* wife and wish the reader to see that they could apply to either in a marital situation.)

SECTION 1
becoming aware

1
dreams about marriage

One reason many marriages are in trouble is because they are based on dreams of living happily ever after, fancy rather than fact, fantasies and fiction rather than reality. The prince and princess do not automatically live happily ever after, the Virginian and the schoolteacher do not marry and ride together into the sunset and bliss.

These dreams do not prepare us for the stark realities of everyday living and marriage. It is the aim of this chapter to explore and explode some of these dreams. In our study, we have found seven major areas on which these dreams seem to focus: love, sex, mate, emotional needs, handling of differences, age, and children.

Dreams About Love

We marry because we love each other. Right? Wrong! Being in love may be a necessary condition for getting married, but it will not keep us married if that is all we have going for us. Most of us have had that romantic feeling about a number of people before we finally settle on the one we will marry. What is the difference? Why does one particular "in love" relationship lead to marriage while others do not? Is it possible that courtship is really a subtle continuing evaluation of whether a relationship will give us what we want and that the romantic "in love" fog is really a smokescreen for a harsh testing and assessment of the other person? In our view and that of others, we would be considered heartless, scheming, and cold were we to admit an inner checklist of our emotional, sexual, social, spiritual, familial, and economic needs against which we measure our prospective partners. Yet this checking goes on continually during courtship.

In olden days, and in some cultures in the present, this choosing was done by the older, cooler heads of parents, relatives, or professional matchmakers. Now, we have the awesome responsibility of choosing our own lifetime partners—a choice sometimes made with all the wisdom of seventeen years of age. Is it any wonder that now there are proponents of serial marriage—a series of spouses to suit us at the various stages of our maturity? Romantic love may be necessary to get us into a marriage, but it is insufficient to keep a marriage going.

Another dream of love is that *love will solve all problems*—love will find a way. We still talk about love as a cure-all, as if this undefined something called love will by magic take care of whatever will come up in the marriage. Unfortunately, life and marriage do not work this way. Most problems are solved through determination, mutual give and take, and respect for each other's feelings (and one's own feelings).

Is love, then, necessary for a good marriage? Of course, but the answer depends on what you call love. If by love you mean something you cannot define because you do not know what it is, then forget it. You do not need love of this kind in marriage. If by love you mean doing unto your mate what you want him or her to do unto you, then, by all means that kind of love is necessary for marriage. However, *love is not enough.* It is the basis on which to begin a marriage. However, the marriage will need more than love to continue. It will need self-respect, self-esteem, and self-hood. By these qualities we mean that a "positive" marriage is based on a positive self. If one's self is negative so will the marriage be.

Marriages are made in heaven. In spite of what we often believe, marriages are made on earth and it is on this earth that marriages can become heaven or hell. Some dreams about marriage and life are necessary to establish goals, as long as these goals are realistic and obtainable. However, if these dreams are to avoid looking at the realities of everyday living, including one's self, reality slips away and trouble begins.

Marriage, then, is like a bridge held up by two pillars. If the pillars are strong, the bridge will weather all sorts of tempests and storms. However, if the pillars are weak, the bridge will collapse. Each of us is one pillar. It is up to each of us to assure that we will be as strong and resilient as we can possibly be.

Dreams About Sex

Sex is the same as love. If this dream means that if you have love, you will also have a good sexual relationship, keep on dreaming. Sex may be better in the safety of a loving relationship. However, the two aspects of marriage are not the same. We can have one without the other; however, in marriage we need both. There are different kinds of love and there are different kinds of sex. It is important that each of us finds out which of them works best for us in our marriage.

By the same token, we expect that our sex life should be perfect from the beginning of our marriage. Such an expectation implies a perfection that is impossible to achieve. Sex needs to be worked on just like any other aspect of the marriage. It is impossible to separate sex from the whole marriage relationship. If we do not get along well out of bed, chances are we will not get along well in bed.

Dreams About the Mate

More often than not we expect our prospective mate to be whatever we feel we are not. If we feel weak, we hope our mate will be strong. If we feel anxious, we hope our mate will be solid and unflappable. If we feel incomplete, we hope our mate will be complete. If we lack confidence, we hope our mate will supply it. In other words, we look for all of the qualities we feel are lacking in us. We select our mate accordingly. Then one day we are in for a rude shock. We find out that our mate is very much like us—scared, uncertain, unclear, and that (s)he was hoping that we had all of the positive qualities (s)he felt lacking in himself or herself! What is the net result? A mutual letdown for both of us! Here the person we hoped would fulfill all of our hopes and dreams has let us down. (S)he is human, anxious, incomplete, scared, and unclear like the rest of us! Who has been fooling whom?

Dreams About Emotional Needs

We all expect that marriage will take care of all or most of our emotional needs for security, happiness, and companionship. We ourselves may not know how to achieve fulfillment of such needs. Yet, we expect our marriage to do what we ourselves cannot do!

Marriage should fulfill all of our human needs. As you can readily see, this dream is putting too much of a burden on a marriage, a burden much greater than any human relationship can take. Although a marriage can and should fulfill some needs, it cannot fulfill all. It is up to each of us to find what we can do to fulfill ourselves and what can or cannot be fulfilled by our marriage. Another aspect of the same dream is that *Marriage will give us happiness.* If you married to escape the unhappiness of your home or the unhappiness of your parents' marriage, then you have taken with you a very heavy burden. This burden may be responsible for the breakup of many marriages because: (a) your past unhappiness did not teach you how to make yourself happy (whatever that may be), and (b) it taught you to expect happiness from *outside* yourself (i.e., from others or from external circumstances). This dream of happiness from the outside of oneself is probably one of the most destructive we can have. No dream could be more false to reality than this one. Happiness, contentment, or whatever you may want to define as satisfaction, comes from one's self, from one's accomplishments, the excitement of behaving positively, from the pleasure of living a productive life. Of course, if you have never experienced these feelings or if no one was there to teach you how to learn being happy, then you would expect this happiness to come from the *outside,* your mate, things, money, status, goods—making happiness dependent on others rather than yourself.

Often we expect that: *Marriage will give happiness to unhappy mates.* If each of us is bringing unhappiness into the marriage, it is very likely that the mate we choose will bring into the marriage just as much unhappiness as we do. How can two unhappy people find happiness together if each of them cannot find it for themselves?

Another need that our marriage should fulfill is that our loneliness will disappear with marriage. Marriage will not cure loneliness, nor will it cure uncertainty, immaturity, unhappiness, feelings of inadequacy, and whatever other negatives each of us may have brought into the marriage. In fact, it is when the marriage is given this function of a cure-all that the marriage is least likely to achieve it.

Dreams About Handling Differences

We expect marriage to be rosy and not marred by anger, frustration, and hurt. If we do not know how to deal with these feelings before marriage, how can we deal with them *in* the marriage?

Differences between males and females cause trouble in marriage. Males are different from females. However, we are also similar in many respects, like membership in the human race, membership in other smaller groups, religious, ethnic groups, socio-economic and neighborhood communities. We can choose to consider differences in our mates as being enhancing of them and of the marriage, or we can choose to see them negatively. For instance, two people from different religious backgrounds or ethnic groups could use the specific characteristics of their group as assets, or the same characteristics can be used as a chance to belittle, put down, and degrade any member of that group. There is nothing innate about these differences that requires that we debase each other.

If you tell your mate to "go to hell," you have a poor marriage. To think that not fighting and not showing hostility is one way of having a happy marriage is inhuman. We all are temperamental, moody, uncertain, fearful, angry, depressed, etc., at times. To deny all of these feelings, including anger, is unrealistic and it is a denial of the very weakness that makes us human. We all are subject to short- or long-lived losses of control. The trick is not to deny such feelings but to express them in the least destructive way we know. No matter how good our intentions may be, we cannot always help getting on each other's nerves. Unfortunately, many of us feel that anger equals rejection and to get angry at people means rejecting them. How about loving and being loved, and occasionally getting angry? Anger has a place in marriage as long as we realize that the love is still there and that all of us need to explode once in a while. In addition, not only is it important to express anger, but more importantly, it is important to share our feelings of hurt, as we shall discuss in a following chapter.

Conflict does not belong in marriage because conflict is bad. Such a dream belongs to people who are afraid to express their feelings, whatever they may be. Under these conditions, no relationship can exist, because if no feelings of any kind are expressed, there is no honesty in the marriage. Conflict is part of our lives. We need to use it to get together, not to set us apart.

Dreams About Age

Anybody above eighteen is ready for marriage. Most of us go into marriage unprepared. Is legal age the same as emotional age? Of course not! Is physical maturity the same as emotional maturity? Of course not!

Our bodies may be more than ready to fulfill each other. However, are our personal dreams and expectations realistic? Are we ready to fulfill the responsibilities required by marriage? Most of us are not. We have received a diploma for graduation from high school. We may have even gone to college and graduated. However, have we ever studied how to be a husband and a wife? We expect that being a married individual will come to us as naturally as breathing and walking. We prepare ourselves for our jobs. Do we prepare ourselves for one of the most responsible jobs ever given to us, the job of being married? Of course not!

Think about the time you have spent to develop a skill, any skill no matter how simple, like driving a car. Did you spend that much time preparing for marriage? Unfortunately, even if you did or wanted to prepare yourself for marriage, you would not find many places where that kind of training is available. Our education takes care of most aspects of life except marriage! Yet we will be married longer and spend more time together married than we will spend on our job!

Dreams About Children

Children will make a marriage better. That is an awful burden to put on the children. They are given the heavy responsibility to save or rescue a poorly conducted marriage. If you hoped that this rescue may happen to your marriage, forget it. You may not believe it now, but wait until those children are growing up and start testing the strength and honesty of your marriage! The dream that *children will improve a marriage* means that if the two of us are unhappy, the birth of a child will provide the happiness we cannot find for ourselves and our marriage. This burden is too great for any child to carry. Under these conditions, the child may well become the bearer of the unhappi-

Dreams About Marriage

ness and the scapegoat of the shortcomings of both mates.

Now that we have gone over this list of dreams, check yourself on it. Check how many of these dreams or beliefs you have held or hold to and check those that you have either given up or never believed in. If you believe about one-third of these dreams your marriage may be in mild trouble. If you still believe about two-thirds of these dreams, your marriage may be in moderate trouble. If you still believe more than two-thirds of these dreams, your marriage may be in severe trouble.

Note: You may not believe any of these dreams, and your marriage may still be in severe trouble or these dreams may have nothing to do with how troubled your marriage is.

Now that we have considered the baggage (or burden?) each of us has taken into the marriage with our dreams, let us determine how troubled our marriage really is, not from the viewpoint of dreams and expectations, but from the viewpoint of how the marriage is working (or not working) for us and our family.

2
checklist for troubled marriages

At this point you may be asking yourself, How deep in trouble am I? Is my marriage troubled or will it survive if I do nothing? Perhaps some guidelines to assess your marriage may be helpful.

If your marriage is satisfying to you, and you and your mate and your children are enjoying each other, and you all together enjoy living, congratulations; you are part of a minority group who may not need books like this. If this, however, is the goal you both—husband and wife—want to reach (that is, enjoying each other and your children) read on.

If you both feel that marriages are made in heaven and that a workable and enjoyable marriage is given free and easy, forget it. Marriages need working on like your car, your house, and your clothes. If you let it go, it will break down and become a nuisance.

What Is Trouble?

Let us understand what is going on in your marriage to see whether you need help. You are both disenchanted and snap at each other easily. Everything that happens in the home is a major crisis. The children are coming between you, and they are succeeding in following the old motto: "Divide and conquer!"

Your fights are increasing in strength and number; and when you are finished, nothing has been achieved and even less solved. You are both going around in circles. Your marriage is now like a broken record. Nothing new is happening, and nothing new is learned. You

Checklist for Troubled Marriages

both get up in the morning with a nagging feeling in the pit of your stomach. You are now questioning whether life is worth living and, even more to the point, whether marriage is all that it is cracked up to be. On the other side of the coin, you may be miles apart from each other. You may not fight, but neither do you talk.

If this is what is going on in your marriage, cheer up! You have company. To get along well and enjoyably all of the time in marriage is the exception. It is not part of the norm! Of course, this realization is not very helpful because you hurt too much.

The degree of trouble in your marriage may depend on whether it is in one area or whether it is in a variety of areas. You may not be aware of trouble in some areas; however, there may be such severe trouble in one area that it may overshadow all the good in other areas. For instance, if all of a sudden you find yourself bankrupt, or in debt, or in jail, or in a hospital, no matter how well all the other areas may work, that one particular incident may trouble all the rest.

However, do not make the mistake of thinking that if that particular trouble had not occurred everything would be dandy! For instance, many families of alcoholics like to think that if it were not for the drinking, everything else in the home would be okay. The family is not willing to consider that that seemingly isolated signal, drinking (or drugs, or bankruptcy, or whatever), is the sign that something is not working in the marriage and in the family. The thinking here is magical: "If it weren't for (name trouble), everything would be okay in our marriage!" If you believe that, you would be making the trouble even more severe. Can you see that that trouble, whatever it may be, tells us that something very serious is going on in your marriage and family that you may not be aware of, and that you cannot see, hear or even admit to yourself? Can you see that that trouble is a signal that false dreams and expectations may have been present, that your awareness of yourself and your behavior may be impaired or limited, that if someone in your family is in trouble you are in just as much trouble as (s)he is? If anyone in the family hurts, everybody else in the family hurts too: that is what marriage and family are all about! We are saying that *where there is trouble, there is hurt, and where there is hurt which is not dealt with properly, there is trouble.*

Self and Marriage

If you married to achieve happiness for yourself, you may have married for the wrong reason. If you expected marriage to make you happy, do not be surprised if you are not. You expected something from marriage that no marriage can do. Marriage cannot give you happiness, because happiness is a very personal decision. Whether each of us is happy or not is up to us. If you married because you were unhappy and thought that marriage would change your unhappiness, you will find that it will not work. Marriage will not change anybody's unhappiness. It may do many, many things and it will give many satisfactions and returns *if you put into it what you are and have.* However, if you were unhappy to begin with and you brought your unhappiness into the marriage, do not expect your marriage to change that unhappiness into happiness for you.

You will find couples who will tell you how happy marriage has made them and how fulfilled they are in their marriage. If they are, consider the possibility that they may have been happy *before* the marriage and that their happiness continued in the marriage. If two unhappy people marry to achieve a state of bliss, one of the many, many dreams about marriage, they will continue to be unhappy and to make each other even more unhappy, since each of them will have let the other down. "I thought *you* were going to make me happy. Since now I am unhappy, it is *your* fault I am still unhappy."

Think about this possibility: Most mates who find each other are very similar to each other in more ways than they may be aware of. Most people who marry deserve each other because they are very much alike in many respects. Therefore, they are very likely to match each other on how unhappy they are. However, they expect the other to provide the happiness they have been unable to achieve themselves. Even more importantly, couples usually match each other in how self-defeating they will be in the marriage. For instance, if one mate deals with his or her feelings through angry explosions, going from one extreme to another of holding in and then letting go suddenly, the other may be constantly nagging or bitching. Both of them may express their feelings in ways that do not help them in the marriage.

Many of us are not aware of how self-defeating we are. However, we are perfectly and painfully aware of how defeating our mate is! If both mates are finding faults in the other, rather than assuming responsibility for their own selves, no wonder the marriage becomes a daily battleground! Both mates expect the other to mend his or her ways, but are unable to see how much they bring into the marriage that is not working. The mote in our mate's eye is clearly visible, but we are unable to see the beam in ours. We are saying that where there is no personal responsibility for one's actions, there is trouble.

By "self-defeating," we mean acting and behaving in ways that get you nothing or get you reactions from others that are unpleasant, frustrating, or not what you would wish. You are left feeling belittled, put down, dissatisfied, and very likely hurt and angry at yourself and others. You may think you have won a battle; however, if your so-called victory is at the expense and loss of those you love, you have defeated yourself.

You are very likely well matched in many, many ways. Or if you think that you are unsuited and different, in fact opposite in many ways, think again. You may differ in how you act, but *both of you* may behave in ways that are self-defeating! If you behave in self-defeating ways, your marriage is just as defeated. How can a bridge stand on weak pillars?

Mildly Troubled Marriages

The checklist that follows is in order of importance and shows what is most important in the long run.

A mildly troubled marriage may go both ways, up or down, depending on what changes take place. A minor adjustment may be all that is necessary. However, if we wait for the marriage to fix itself, we may have to wait a long, long time! We are now going to consider various areas of the marriage that may need looking at and evaluating.

Self

There may not be serious trouble except for boredom, tiredness of the same daily routine, dissatisfaction with little things, occasional temper outbursts, some worry and nervousness, occasional sleepless nights, little pleasure in living, some feeling of emptiness, and questions like Who am I? What do I want from life? may remain unanswered.

Mate

Your mate may be giving you indirect signs and signals of dissatisfaction. (S)he shows some of the same signs noted above or may be somewhat withdrawn, untalkative, moody, uninterested, distant, and somewhat unreachable. If you try to discuss the situation, however, you may get a sharp denial, "What are you talking about?" or "You have been reading too many books lately," or "You have been watching too many TV shows," etc.

Marriage

The relationship between you and your mate may be going along with a certain degree of repetition, tiring sameness, little excitement or pleasure, and some emptiness. The marriage may be limping along, but it does not seem to have the same zing—the same interest it had in the past. It may show some of the following features:

(1) Occasional spats repeating and rehashing unpleasant parts of past events, including the courtship and honeymoon.
(2) Interference from parents or in-laws in your marriage.
(3) Interference from your children.
(4) Poor or infrequent sex.
(5) Little or no enjoyment of life, limited going out, no entertainment, and if and when vacation or leisure time is available, inadequate use of them.
(6) Avoidance of confronting issues (financial, sexual, child-raising problems, etc.).

Other areas of trouble may be:

Mixed-up Priorities

For instance, the provider is spending too much time and energy at his/her work. The housekeeper is too involved in raising the children.

Children

They get along without too many crises except for occasional fights and sassiness, or spats with you, your mate or others. They assume their responsibilities; however, there may be one area where they neglect such responsibilities, i.e., their manners or taking care of their clothes, room, homework, household chores, or school grades.

Parents or In-Laws

Even though they may be self-sufficient, they may have been bothersome at times, putting one of you down in your roles as a mate or a parent. They may still consider you their little child and you may be helping them along by behaving like a little child toward them. The umbilical cord may not have yet been cut!

Friends

Your range of friends may be limited by the fact that you have many acquaintances but few friends. It is hard during a lifetime to have more than a handful of close friends. That means that both you and your mate have been able to find other couples who are similar in many ways to you in sharing interests, education, and enjoyment. If you have few enjoyable friends or are not considered enjoyable by other couples, you may want to start asking yourself why. With close friends you can talk about anything under the sun and you are not afraid to let them know where you are at any given time in your life. If you do not have friends with whom you can be yourself freely, it is time to start wondering.

Work

Under this category one should consider at least three different kinds of work: (a) household chores, (b) the job, and (c) school. Is there any trouble in any one of these three areas?

Are household chores being postponed and not taken care of? Are the home and its surroundings going downhill without anyone doing anything about it? Are painting, gardening, and cleaning up accepted parts of the *shared* responsibilities in the home? Are there ongoing hassles about who should do what, when and where, while nothing is accomplished?

Is the job a source of pleasure and satisfaction, or is it just a job, something to be done with no pride, no pleasure, and yes, not even pain? How committed is the provider or jobholder in the home to making the job a source of personal satisfaction? Is the job dull, routine, uninteresting, unpleasant, and a source of discord brought home? If the answer to these questions as a whole is yes, trouble may be ahead.

Is the school starting to be a "pain in the neck"? Poor grades, poor conduct, too many teacher conferences, principal calling with perhaps one area of learning which is below what your child should be able to accomplish? Is school like household chores and the job—another of those pains we all need to endure? Or is it a source of pleasure, excitement, healthful competition, and growth?

Finances

The amount of money made is less important than how it is spent. If money is a source of worry, complaints, or fights, start thinking about the expectations you may have about money. Is it being used to help the family or in ways hurtful to the family? Is money never enough because no concrete, realistic planning and budget have been worked out? Have you and your mate sat down and worked out a budget? Do each of you know where and how the money is spent? Is it spent responsibly (for the family) or irresponsibly (for the self without consideration of others)? We live in a very seductive, enticing society that has given us quick, easy credit and has encouraged us to buy, buy, buy before we have earned the money. We are enticed and encouraged to buy without thinking about interest rates, taxes, hidden charges, etc. If you have fallen into this trap and you are deep into it, what are you planning to do to get out of it?

Free Time

What does the family do with its spare time? Does it enjoy itself and seek to move out, go places, work constructively to do and learn something new, or is the family collapsed before the television set, doing nothing, going nowhere, failing to use weekends, evenings and vacations to their fullest? How is free time used: (a) inside the home, (b) outside the house (for instance, repairs or gardening), (c) in the neighborhood, (d) in the community (church membership, organizations, activities, etc.)?

On the other hand, is the spare time so much taken up by

Checklist for Troubled Marriages

activities that no time for reflection, rest, and just doing nothing is available? Doing too much can be just as destructive as doing too little. Have you found that middle of the road that works best for your marriage?

Moderately Troubled Marriages

Moderate trouble is present in a marriage if there is trouble in several (if not all) of the areas listed above. In other words, just mild trouble in most areas may add up to moderate trouble. In addition, the following conditions may be present:

Self

Some excessive, self-destructive habits may be present and you cannot prevent yourself from doing them, such as overeating, oversmoking, overdrinking, overworking, overgambling, etc. Occasional sleepless nights have turned into more chronic sleeplessness. You may be shirking your assigned responsibilities either at home or at work, withdrawing from social contacts, putting down and being critical of others, especially your mate, to the point of nagging, complaining, and exploding repeatedly from your personal unhappiness.

Mate

Some of the signs noted above are also present in your mate. Your bringing them up is taken as a personal putdown or is the signal for a bitter fight and loss of temper for both of you.

Marriage

The time spent together is taken up by unpleasant discussions, bitter accusations, and even occasional physical abuse. By the same token, you may not fight, being polite with each other but distant and far from each other emotionally.

In addition to the possible problems mentioned above, two additional qualities need to be considered in this category: (a) intensity; and (b) frequency. Is fighting too intense and too frequent? On the other hand, if you are avoiding each other, not getting together sexually, physically, or emotionally, to the point of little or no contact or concern, then your marriage may be in just as much trouble as extreme fighting.

Children

One of your children is by now a "black sheep" by having become either a bully or passive, withdrawn, and unsociable. School problems and learning difficulties are now extended beyond the early grades and are not going away.

Parents or In-Laws

One of you is still so involved with his or her parents that considerable time, money, and effort is given to them or their importance is given such a position that your marriage and children are second.

Friends

Your circle of friends and acquaintances is limited. Your friends are unable to give you what you need when you need it. You have trouble socializing and enjoying your friends. Occasionally you have trouble with your neighbors and you seem unable to make friends among coworkers or in your neighborhood, church, and community. Your children may be unable to do better than you are doing or their choice of friends is not to your liking.

Work

In either one of the three areas (a) household chores, (b) the job, and (c) school, there is or has been a breakdown, like a sudden firing at work, piling up of household chores not completed, or suspension from school.

Finances

You may be in debt and have trouble paying off all the creditors. It may be that one of you takes the role of the self-indulgent spendthrift, while the other assumes the position of the self-sacrificing martyr who puts everyone else's material needs (new shoes, new fishing rod, etc.) ahead of his or her own.

Free Time

You find little free time to spend together. You may be busy with a lot of activities, all of which take you away from your mate or family. On the other hand, you may all be together (watching TV, etc.) but never making contact or enjoying each other's presence.

Seriously Troubled Marriage

The points made earlier are already present, but in addition:

Self

Your unhappiness may be so severe that you are now using crutches like drugs prescribed by a physician, or have taken refuge in excessive religious fervor, using your religion as a magic wand, or you may have fallen into apathy, despair, giving up and withdrawing. You are no longer in charge of yourself and let others (family, community, agencies, professionals) take care of you.

Mate

What you are experiencing in a troubled marriage will also be troubling your mate. However, the way that the unhappiness is shown may be different from your expression of unhappiness. You may be overeating, for instance, while your mate may be running around or may have violated in one way or another the legal or moral limits set by society.

Marriage

You may be so estranged from each other that there may be no contact or communication and the little there is may be destructive. Sex by now may be mechanical or joyless. It may no longer be a reciprocal act but the exploitation of the other for physical release or it may have been given up entirely.

Little or no warmth, affection, or understanding is felt or expressed to one another.

Children

One or more of your children is now out-of-control to the point that the law or other community agencies, in addition to the school, have become involved. He may be a nuisance in the neighborhood, and you get frequent complaints from the neighbors.

Parents or In-Laws

They may be living with you or you with them and instead of helping one another you are at each other's throats. They may have become an emotional or financial drag on you and may be a source of constant bickering. Loyalty to one's parents may be expressed in ways that are at the expense of one's mate or children.

Friends

You may be living isolated in the community, or if you have had friends, you may no longer keep in touch with them. If there are friends, they may be his friends to fish, hunt, golf, or play poker with or her friends to play bridge, shop, or gossip with, but never the twain shall meet—there are no friends held in common.

Work

One or both of you may have serious job problems—changing jobs frequently, getting bored, or being extremely dissatisfied. In terms of your advancement or earning a livelihood, you are running very fast to stand still or even to fall behind.

Rather than taking pleasure in one's surroundings, household chores are left undone to the level of mere survival.

One or more of your children is falling down in his job—which is school work. He may be failing or he may drop out.

Finances

Gross mismanagement may have led to nonpayment of bills or rent with consequent harassment of creditors or eviction. In extreme cases the financially troubled family may no longer be self-supporting and may need outside help like welfare.

Free Time

There is no free time for the marriage and the family together, for frequently in seriously troubled marriages, energy is wasted in non-constructive activities, antisocial acts, or is just frittered away. There is no pleasure in free time.

The Meaning of Trouble

Are there criteria for satisfaction and contentment in life? Yes, there are ways in which we can tell the difference between a satisfactory and unsatisfactory marriage. In fact, not only can we distinguish between degrees of trouble, but we can also distinguish between degrees of satisfaction and contentment. Being happy in no way means that we are trouble-free. On the contrary, we cannot live and not be troubled. However, what matters is how we cope and deal with trouble when it comes.

To help check on the degree of trouble in your marriage, it may be helpful to check on the degree of satisfaction. Therefore, we want to distinguish between average and ideal marriages and mildly, moderately, and seriously troubled marriages. The more troubled, the greater the amount of help needed.

The Causes of Trouble

All too often we want to find the causes for our troubles. That search is fine and good if it works for improved understanding and change in our marriage. On the other hand, it may be a waste of time.

We could spend a great deal of time finding out culprits, reasons, and causes. However, be sure if you embark in this search that you do not use these so-called causes to label your spouse, your parents, one of your children, or someone outside of your marriage as the "guilty" person to blame for all your troubles. All of the external targets may be convenient ways of avoiding dealing with yourself and your marriage. It is comfortable to blame our troubles on others. In this way we do not have to change. It is the other guys who must change.

If you spend a great deal of time finding "causes" in your past, watch out; you may be spending your time in the past to avoid dealing with the present or the future. If you look for someone to blame, to pin the "cause" on, give it up. Each of us is responsible for what happens to our marriage. Eventually the search for causes external to ourselves may cause even more trouble to those we love and, therefore, to ourselves. Eventually we need to look at ourselves as human beings with a present and a future. If as human beings we are lacking or incomplete, the partnership will be lacking and incomplete and our parenting will be too.

The most common source of trouble, which may reach serious proportions, is the messed up priorities, which consist of mother taking care of children, father involved in his work, and never the two getting together. Being wholly involved either in children or work becomes a socially acceptable way to avoid looking at the marriage.

In other words, being partners is given up for being a "good mother" or being a "good provider." If this is the case with you, be very careful; it may mean that both of you may be incomplete as human beings and you are trying to be "good" parents or providers to make up for not feeling good in being human and being partners.

Ideal Marriage

Perhaps our discussion would not be complete without some illustration of what an optimal, "ideal" marriage *could* be like. In the first place, optimal marriages are *not* made in heaven, they are made on earth. It takes a great deal of commitment, maturity, flexibility, compassion, and responsibility to make such a union, so much so that it is almost impossible to define this ideal. The ideal use of the marital relationship means mutual enhancement in whatever is done and said with no letdown or putdown of anyone else. It means providing for ourselves and one another in an atmosphere in which we are free to feel good about ourselves and about each other. It means a relationship in which we are our best selves. How many of us can reach this level?

The ideal marriages, despite the many different types, do show some important common characteristics: Shared leadership in a democratic sort of way, closeness, effectiveness in negotiations, clarity in expression of feelings and thoughts, acceptance of personal responsibility for one's words and deeds, open expression and acceptance of opinions, and complementarity in each other's problem-solving and decision-making. One of the best characteristics of this type of marriage is a positive attitude toward life. To this quality one should add mutual respect, flexibility and spontaneity, and initiative in starting new projects or new ways of looking at things.

Average Marriage

An adequate working marriage does not mean that everything is "hunky-dory" or "peachy-keen." On the contrary, the "usual" or "average" marriage represents an extremely wide range of various marriages that may be very different from each other. Their major common characteristic, however, is that they are working, producing, and useful. Both partners in the marriage feel satisfied and serene, feel they are getting what they want from their marriage, and they use it to deal with their own selves, their children, and their in-laws and to cope with the world. It works so that the partners are together in most decisions, are able to compromise, to give and take, and to reach decisions that are mutually beneficial.

In this marriage both partners complement each other without opposing each other. This means that even though they may differ on a variety of issues they do not use their differences as weapons with which to hit each other over the head. They accept and deal with these differences as representing the individuality of each partner, without seeing these differences as sources of conflict, tension, and acrimony. In other words, in this kind of marriage the partners are able to live with and at times reconcile their differences without becoming bitter enemies. Each partner is able to hold on to himself and not become a lesser human being than he was on entering the marriage.

Now that we have described what adequately working and ideal marriages may look like, we may be better ready to distinguish among three different degrees of trouble: Mild, moderate, and serious.

Mildly Troubled Marriage

There may be one single issue that presents itself again and again and does not seem to go away, such as overeating in one marriage partner or some other mild excess, or a deficit in one of the children, as underachievement. Or the deficit may be in one of the partners, like refusing to socialize or make friends.

In the mildly troubled marriage the trouble is isolated and no other troubles are apparent. The trouble repeats itself and is apparent more than once or twice. If any trouble appears only once, do not worry. On the other hand, you could have a series of different little troubles that may add up to one big problem—trouble shows itself in different ways at different times. Big or small, you need to consider what that trouble does to your marriage—does it enhance it or does it belittle it? Does this trouble provide a chance to talk it over or is it the cause of further conflict and withdrawal for the both of you? How do you both use trouble? Do you use it to hit each other over the head or do you use it to get together more often and better? All of these considerations are important at any level of trouble and both of you need to consider what trouble *means*. Is it isolated or does it crop up too often for comfort? What are the results of the trouble? Is it an occasion for negotiation and improvement or is it the occasion for more deterioration in your marriage?

In adequate or mildly troubled marriages, there is a thin line between satisfaction and contentment arising out of reality and living in a fool's paradise. There may be contentment based on reality and then there may be contentment and satisfaction from wearing blinders over one's eyes. In other words, the satisfaction may be based on a denial of the realities that keep staring us in the face but which we chose to deny the existence as problems. For instance, we could deny that drinking one or two drinks a day is a problem. However, if it affects our health and our paying attention to our mate and to the rest of the family, those two innocent little drinks may produce more trouble than they are worth. The behavior may not be troublesome to you, like smoking a cigarette, but the smoke may go into other eyes (and lungs?). Trouble starts right there on the relationship between our innocent innocuous behavior and how others around us choose to react to it. The same applies to how we react to the innocent and and seemingly safe behavior of others. How we react to each other is the source of the problem.

Moderately Troubled Marriage

The trouble may be isolated (or specific) or may not be too intense. However, if it repeats itself and becomes increasingly intense or stronger, then it may have reached the moderate stage. For instance, most people drink here and there. However, if drinking starts to become a pattern and occurs more often than just on social or special occasions, it may reach dangerous proportions. If it reaches the "stoned" or "blank" stage even *once,* the trouble is by now no longer mild, it is at best moderate. If it is not dealt with right now, and if it does not decrease or stop, it may get worse. Other examples could be coming home late, flirting at parties, neglecting the upkeep of the home, or any other behavior that reaches troublesome proportions. Its frequency (how often it takes place) and its intensity (how severe is it?) are the two important questions that only you can answer. If the habit is now a pattern that repeats itself often and

Checklist for Troubled Marriages

strongly enough to cause you unhappiness, dissatisfaction, shame, guilt, embarrassment, extra expense, extra time with no results to show for your efforts either inside or outside of you, the trouble may now be moderate. It may have come to the point of affecting external areas: at work (the boss), at school (the principal), at the bank (the balance), in the courthouse, in the neighborhood, your in-laws, your friends, your church. Do you want it to become serious?

Seriously Troubled Marriage

The list of checks for serious trouble are easier than in any of the previous categories. Your marriage is in serious trouble when the trouble impinges on the external areas listed above more than once. Your physician may ask for consultation with a psychiatrist or psychologist, your child is in trouble with the law or juvenile authorities, lawyers and courts are involved. Whatever the trouble, it manifests itself by extending outside of your home. At this point, there may not be much to be done. Usually marriages in serious trouble stay that way without changing, except for the worse. At this level, what may have seemed defeats at the mild and moderate levels have become destruction, someone in your house is being destroyed, there may be murder, suicide, hospitalization, arrest, or other extreme situations present.

At this stage, the marriage may be beyond rescue. You may be so shocked and shaken by the sheer task of survival that it may be impossible for you to do anything constructive. Destruction may become so intense and pervasive that nothing constructive can be done at this point. If this is the point your marriage or your family has reached, ask yourself if this is what you want out of life and whether the destruction can be turned into construction. If you really want to do something about your troubles, no matter how serious, you can still do it. With determination, there is always hope.

Rules of Thumb: Three general rules of thumb to judge for trouble in your marriage are as follows:

Mild: All of you (parents, children, and in-laws) are able to function outside of the home but you are not getting on well *inside* the home.

Moderate: One or more of you is not getting on well *outside* the home, *in addition* to your not getting on *inside* the home. However, the trouble is limited, either in the job or the school or the neighborhood.

Serious: One or more of your family has gotten caught in a community agency (jail, bankruptcy court, juvenile authorities, thrown out of school, etc.) It means you are not getting along either outside or inside your home.

3
more checks

Can you be troubled without your marriage being in trouble? Or, to put it another way, can you still be unhappy even though your marriage seems to be working all right? It could be; that is, there is the possibility that you may still be unhappy even though your mate is perfectly contented and satisfied with the marriage. You will need his or her help to find out what is troubling you and what you can do to improve your lot in life. Since any change you make in your life will very likely affect your mate, (s)he may as well be a part of the change. In the process of your changing, your mate may find better ways of understanding and changing himself (or herself) for his own good. Since you want to share whatever the marriage gives, you will want to share your unhappiness with your mate; you will want your mate also to share in the process of leaving behind your unhappiness and searching for new happiness. If you are together in this search, your marriage can grow stronger and better.

One way of pinpointing causes of unhappiness in one partner is to examine the priorities in one's life and the mutual priorities of the couple. In addition to ordering the priorities in our lives, each of us has parts we play which will get us and the ones we love absolutely nothing in the way of happiness. "Getting hooked" is another way of getting a marriage in trouble. Let us consider priorities, parts, and "getting hooked" in detail.

Priorities

You may not be able to find any trouble area suggested in the previous chapter. However, there may be trouble in the priorities which have been set. For instance, both of you may have agreed that work or the job is so important that work comes first and the marriage second. Or else you could have tacitly agreed that the children are more important than the marriage, that is, children come first and marriage second.

Priorities Inside the Family

There are four major aspects to a family which need to be continuously kept in balance: (1) self, (2) marriage, (3) children, and (4) parents or in-laws. All of these in one way or another are necessary for emotional survival. However, the order of importance—how one will be balanced in relationship to the others—is basic to the survival of the marriage. If the children are given a position ahead of the marriage, the marriage will not survive. If loyalty to parents or in-laws is primary, the marriage will not survive. And if in these cases the marriage does survive, it will be a sorry, limping, crippled thing.

If your priorities are mixed up, the marriage is in trouble. Another type of mix-up relates to putting marriage ahead of the self. Couple after couple coming into our office suffers from the common hang-up of wanting to make their mate happy. They have the altogether self-defeating dream that part of marriage is to make the *other,* the mate, happy by sacrificing themselves and their own needs. How can we make our mate happy if we do not know how to do it for ourselves?

This mix-up points to the fact that making oneself happy is the *first priority* to consider *provided* that making oneself happy is *not* done at the expense of the mate. If our mate has to pay a price for our happiness it will not work!

Think of how the family has come about: One individual self meeting and marrying another individual self. The marriage is a third entity, the product of these two selves who then have to deal with their children and with their parents and in-laws. Eventually in the usual course of events, the parents or in-laws will die. This loss needs to be shared by the whole family, because eventually the children will also leave, although not so finally as the grandparents. What is left? The marriage and the two selves of the mates. It is at this point that a great many divorces take place because the marriage was given up or shunted to a lower position for the children's sake. When the children leave, the marital relationship may be too weak to last. This is the reason why we feel children should be kept in third place in the list of priorities. This position, of course, in no way belittles or denies their importance. It only helps us achieve a perspective of where they belong in relationship to the rest of the family.

Once the mates are left by themselves, after the children have gone on to make lives of their own, one of them in the course of time will die. What is left? The individual self of the surviving mate. If the survivor has given up his or her self for the sake of the marriage, it will be very difficult to go on living. In fact, one of the peak periods of suicide in older people occurs within a year of the loss of the mate. If there is no suicide, there is a great deal of depression and need for medical and psychiatric attention.

Priorities Outside the Family

While the priorities inside the family are important for emotional survival of the self, as we have already noted, priorities outside of the family are important for the physical and economic survival of the self and of the family. It is clear that work is necessary to get money and to buy the necessities and even luxuries of life. Work, therefore, and what it provides, money, is necessary for material survival. Very often work and material survival are put ahead of emotional survival. Success on the job, high school achievement, or social success or popularity are examples of other priorities that may be confused and oftentimes put ahead of emotional survival. When this confusion takes place and work is put ahead of one's family, the marriage is endangered or at the very least put in jeopardy. The one who works and provides the material goods may become so taken by this responsibility that the importance of emotional survival takes second place to economic survival. If and when this imbalance takes place, it puts a great deal of stress on the marriage.

Other kinds of intangible priorities, like power, achievement, and acquiring of knowledge, or accumulation of goods, like money-making, may take priority over emotional goods, like affection, trust, caring, and all other qualities that are important for emotional survival. Investment in this kind of goods can be as deadly to the marriage as too much investment in the search for material goods.

It is important, therefore, for us to think about priorities, both the emotional and the material. Think whether you and your mate have kept them in the proper balance and perspective. If you have, your marriage should be in good shape. If you have not, your marriage may be in trouble.

In addition to the relative balance or imbalance of priorities in the family, you need to think about the parts that are played in the family. Can you recognize any of these?

Parts

We do know that there are at least four definite parts that are destructive to the marriage. These parts may sound somewhat ridiculous. However, the effects they can have on the marriage can be troublesome. These parts are played this way.

Martyrs

This person feels that (s)he has to bear a cross all of his or her life for past sins and mistakes. In men, this part is played by being *Casper Milktoasts,* and in women, it is played by being long-suffering heroines, trying to please everybody, being the peacemaker, avoiding fights and anger, being overly nice, and thereby accomplishing absolutely nothing!

Movie Stars

This individual is always doing something, even though whatever he may be doing has nothing to do with the marriage. Men in this part play *Cowboys,* being always on the go, cooking important deals, and getting nowhere. Women play the part of *Barbie Dolls,* spending a great deal of time making themselves cute but doing nothing to help themselves and the marriage. When the big hat for the boys and the makeup for the girls no longer work, there is only emptiness left.

Robots

This part is played with the head. Men play this part as *Comput-*

ers since they *know* that logic and knowledge is enough to solve all human problems. They will have solid, logical solutions that solve absolutely nothing, since most of our problems are human and deal mainly with *how we feel* and not with *how we think*. In this part, the Computer thinks but does not do, while the Cowboy does but does not think. Women in this part play *Ann Landers*. They have read all the self-help books they can find and *know* what to do. Unfortunately, they seem to be unable to put into action all their knowledge!

Patriots

Disagreeing and blaming others is the way this part is played. Men are *Superpatriots,* that is, they know exactly what is "right" (which makes anybody else "wrong"), and they are quick to point out faults in others (but not in themselves). Women act like *Amazons* or worse, *Harpies,* charging with battleaxes, cutting down everybody in their wake. They use sex as a weapon, cannot forget past deeds supposedly done to them, and are quick to find that others rather than themselves are responsible for whatever trouble they may have.

Men and women can exchange parts. Some switch from one to another. However, each of these parts can be deadly to the marriage. If one plays a part, it forces the mate to play another part. In this way both mates get away from being human beings.

Getting Hooked

By "getting hooked," we mean the escalation that takes place when one of us is upset. The upset in one of us becomes a signal for upset in the other. As a result, what started as a minor incident or accident becomes a major event, just because one of the two chose to become upset rather than to ignore the incident. Just because one of us behaves like a so-and-so is no reason for the other to do likewise. However, such getting hooked implies that both of us have become so fused with each other that neither one of us knows where one ends and the other begins. Neither one of us can stand aside and say: "That's upsetting him. However, just because he is upset it does not mean I have to be upset." The knack of keeping oneself separate, although sympathetic, and not escalating an upset in one's partner is difficult to acquire in a troubled marriage, but it is essential if the marriage is not to deteriorate into a broken, repetitious record of constant bickering which never leads to a resolution.

Putting It All Together

Now you should be able to rate your marriage. Check each item in Table I for your degree of satisfaction. After each of you has checked the list, discuss it with your mate. See how you agree or disagree on any of these items. If you are able to talk about all of these points and are able to recognize what needs to be done, maybe your marriage is okay.

If while you discuss these points you find: (a) that you disagree on how each of you sees the point in question and (b) that you are getting angrier and angrier or frustrated in not being able to find some degree of agreement, your marriage may be in trouble. Set an appointment with each other in a week to (a) think more calmly about all these issues, and (b) consider possible ways of getting out of the rut you may be in. If you cannot iron out your differences, you may need to read on. Please note that although filling out this checklist may seem dull and unnecessary, it may also provoke some fear in you. What if you indeed find, after you rate your marriage, that it is in trouble? How much easier it is to deny, avoid, and bury one's head in the sand when some danger arises. Avoiding and denying trouble, however, is not a way of making it go away. In fact, the more you deny trouble, the more trouble you may have! Hence, we would suggest that considering this checklist is the best way to avoid trouble. Perhaps for the first time in your life you may be able to look at yourself and your marriage squarely. That, of course, is not easy to do. You have our encouragement to try.

One word of caution about this checklist. Not all items have the same value and weight. Some items, for instance, like church or community activities, may be more important to some or less important to others. Each item in and by itself may not count. It is the overall impression, the summing up of all the various aspects of your marriage that counts. No single item in the checklist, no matter how negative, can be given the burden of telling you whether your marriage is in trouble. It will take more than one item to conclude whether your marriage is troubled or not.

TABLE I / *Marriage Checklist*

Degree of Satisfaction

	Very High	High	So-So	Low	Very Low	Trouble Mild	Trouble Mod	Trouble Sev
Self								
Dreams								
Mate								
Marriage								
Children								
Parents								
In-Laws								
Friends								
Work								
House								
Job								
School								
Finances								
Free Time								
Evenings								
Weekends								
Church								
Holidays								
Vacations								
Hobbies								
Neighbors								
Civic Groups								
Priorities								
Inside Family								
Outside Family								
Getting Hooked								
Parts								
Martyr								
Milktoast								
Heroine								
Movie Star								
Cowboy								
Doll								
Patriot								
Superpatriot								
Amazon								
Robot								
Computer								
Ann Landers								

TABLE I / *Marriage Checklist*

Degree of Satisfaction

	Very High	High	So-So	Low	Very Low	Trouble Mild	Trouble Mod	Trouble Sev
Self								
Dreams								
Mate								
Marriage								
Children								
Parents								
In-Laws								
Friends								
Work								
House								
Job								
School								
Finances								
Free Time								
Evenings								
Weekends								
Church								
Holidays								
Vacations								
Hobbies								
Neighbors								
Civic Groups								
Priorities								
Inside Family								
Outside Family								
Getting Hooked								
Parts								
Martyr								
Milktoast								
Heroine								
Movie Star								
Cowboy								
Doll								
Patriot								
Superpatriot								
Amazon								
Robot								
Computer								
Ann Landers								

SECTION 2
what are the possibilities?

4
how do marriages become troubled?

The most important questions you need to ask are: How did your marriage get into trouble? The second important question is: How did I contribute to the trouble? Very likely you are using a lot of energy and time in putting the blame on your mate for the trouble you are in. Let us pursue this line of thought to see where it leads.

(1) As long as you blame and complain about your mate, your mate can do the same. If both of you continue to blame and complain about each other, you will be spinning your wheels. No one can win in this situation. No new information will be exchanged, since it has all been said before.

(2) As long as your thought and energy are given to figuring out the wrongdoings of your mate, you will have little time left to think about what *you* are doing that is not paying off for you and your marriage. Blaming takes time and thought away from yourself: you cannot think about yourself and blame your mate at the same time. The use of the pronoun "you" can be one of the most destructive acts in a marriage if it is used to blame, to finger-point, and to find fault.

(3) If you think that your mate is "more at fault" than you, forget it. In the first place, it is not a matter of fault but one of responsibility. In the second place, it took two of you to make a marriage and it took two of you to make it troubled.

The only possible contribution you can make to the situation is to start answering the questions: "What am I doing that is not working? How can I stop doing what is not paying off for me and what can

I do to make things better for me?" If you cannot come up with answers to these questions you are in serious trouble, for, you have put the responsibility for your life on your mate, and by thinking about him or her you have avoided looking at yourself.

Investing Energy in Defeat

Our energy can be invested in changing ourselves or in staying the same. If one of you is beginning to invest in changing, and if both of you have defined yourselves by opposition to each other, it is clear that one mate will oppose the mate who wants change. How will he oppose? By not wanting any change, of course!

Perhaps we should say more about opposing each other as mates, which is one of the more frequent patterns found in troubled marriages. Most of us learn to oppose our parents when we are children, especially if our parents set themselves up to be opposed. If parents demand of their child conformity to their wishes and commands and in so doing take all self-determination away from the child, the only choices for the child are either obey and conform and lose self-determination or oppose, rebel, disobey, and learn to determine oneself *through opposition*. Therefore, if we have learned to define ourselves *in opposition* to our parents, it is very likely that we will carry over such a pattern into our marriage. As a matter of fact, if we have learned to define ourselves through opposition, we will very likely choose as a partner someone who has used exactly the same pattern! As a result, marriage becomes a matter of two individuals, supposedly adults, who oppose each other as parent and child!

Once this extremely negative pattern—opposition—is established in marriage, it is very difficult to change. If and when one mate wants to do something positive, it is clear that the other mate will oppose it by doing something negative. Consequently, the only positive effect that can result may be when both agree that *both* need change. If they have agreed to disagree with each other, change is not possible.

How Self-Defeating Can We Be?

Proving It

Will one of you have to *prove* to the other that your marriage needs improving? Does one of you have to take the whole burden for changes in your marriage? If it is a partnership, both of you need to be in touch with each other so that each of you knows where your mate is physically, mentally, and *emotionally*. If one of you needs to prove that something is not working in your marriage, then your marriage is in trouble, since it means that one of you is not in touch and is not listening to the other.

How many depressed mates have we seen who need to *do* something highly destructive to convince the other mate that there is a problem? How many acting-out mates have we seen who go to all sorts of self-defeating extremes to bring home the message: Our marriage is not working well? How many children have been made the scapegoats of unhappy and destructive marriages?

Confronting Oneself

Let us make clear what we are talking about. When we talk about marriage we are talking about an *emotional* relationship between two human beings. When we talk about this relationship and about changing it for the better, *we are talking about how each of you feels about himself and about the other.* Therefore, we are talking about *feelings.* If one of you avoids dealing with your feelings, it is natural that the other will not want to get in touch with how he feels. If feelings have been avoided over a long period, change will be difficult. Change in oneself means change in how one feels about oneself and one's marriage. If one of you says: "I want change," it requires doing one of the most difficult things we can do, that is, looking into ourselves and how we feel! People go to great lengths to avoid getting in touch with their feelings. They will kill themselves, kill others, get drunk, get married, change jobs, change mates, and do many other destructive things to avoid getting in touch with those feelings. Some of us have built such walls around these feelings and are so comfortable with the way those walls are working that we do not want any change under any condition, even if it means divorce. Now one of us wants to change this state of things. It will be difficult.

Can you see what we are talking about? In order for a marriage to change it requires doing something we may have never done before! How can anyone demand so much? Many marriages continue through life without a legal divorce. However, the emotional divorce is there and it pleases both partners because both partners are in agreement to avoid closer or deeper intimacy.

Even in couples who have been married many years and who have proudly made a success of their marriage, there may be an emotional atrophy. There is accomodation, not confrontation. There is adjustment, not intimacy. There is compromise, not improvement. It is no wonder that many marriages go stale after a number of years.

Considering Choices

You may, understandably, feel that no choices are available to you. Divorce seems the only way out of an impossible situation. The marriage seems unworkable and unrewarding to both of you. Why? Let us examine the reasons.

Hurting and Fighting

Hurt and conflict in marriage are a blessing and an asset. Hurt is the ultimate proof of caring. If you both hurt, it means that you both care for the marriage. Hurt in marriage and life is inevitable. Usually hurt comes from those who care for us (our parents) and from those we care for (our mate and our children). If there is no care, there is no hurt. Hence, consider your hurt an asset. If you both care enough to hurt, you may care enough to seek and work for a better marriage. We are really doubtful whether care, commitment, and communication are present if there is no hurt and pain. In fact, you may consider all of your problems as unsuccessful ways of dealing with your own internal hurt.

When we speak of hurt we are speaking of human, personal, non-physical hurt. Some psychologists called it "psychic suffering." It is a feeling that sometimes may well reach physical proportions. However, most of the time it is a feeling closely related to helplessness, a feeling of worthlessness, anxiety, fear, and a host of negative, unpleasant, and painful emotions. That hurt can be used to destroy your marriage and your family, or you can use that hurt to seek more positive ways of helping yourself and your marriage. How do you want to use that hurt? Positively or negatively, constructively or destructively, helpfully or hurtfully? That is your choice, and no one can make that choice for you.

The hurt you feel can be used destructively by piling pain and hurt on top of pain and hurt, or it can be used constructively by avoiding making the same mistakes twice. That hurt can change your marriage for the worse or for the better. You can decide to have a lousy marriage and be part of it through commissions or omissions, or you can decide to have a better marriage by working on it. If you continue in a lousy marriage, you must be enjoying it.

Either-Or Thinking

One trouble with hurt is the tricks it plays on our thinking. Under pressure, stress, and pain, we start thinking in either-or terms. That is, we either stay married or we divorce. No solution in between appears possible. If we cannot get along married, let us break it up. This either-or thinking, unfortunately, is at the bottom of a great deal of destructive behavior: we are either weak or strong, nothing in between. Examples of hurtful either-or talking and thinking are the following:

"Either we are happy or we are not."
"Either we stay married or we do not."
"Either you change or I will not stay married to you."
"Either you talk to me or I will throw a dish at you."

Another aspect of either-or talk is the use of "always" or "never," especially in blaming and accusing our partner: "You *never* talk to me." "You *always* walk away when I want to talk to you." "You *never* really cared for me."

Under either-or conditions, we start using all-or-nothing labels that deny our many human assets and our inner, integral selfhood. These labels rob us of our humanity, and, under stress, we use them on each other liberally, fluently, and frequently. Name-calling is usually related to either-or thinking and the attempt (usually fruitless) to keep the one-up position on the other. It stems from the foolish idea that one's victories are based on the other's losses. If this is another game you are practicing—"I win, you lose"—good luck to you! If one of you wins at the other's expense, it is doubtful whether anybody is winning at all. One's loss cancels the other's win.

Under stress and strain, under the daily pressures of mutual humiliation and reciprocal put-downs, no creative or constructive choices seem available to you. You have already parted company. You have already reached the point of seeing yourselves according to extremes. One of you is the "bad guy" and the other the "good guy." One of you is the oppressor and the other the oppressed. One of you is the murderer and the other the victim. Each of you is an enemy to the other one. Do you see how either-or thinking works? How can there be solutions when each of you is all black or all white, all bad or all good? Under either-or thinking, no constructive solutions are possible.

Either-or thinking is the type of thinking that through history has made foes of friends: "Either you are with me or you are against me." We remember a couple, both of whom were college graduates. He had a professional degree and she was helping him in the office. Their time was spent bickering on how he was "good" and she was "bad." He spent all of his energy proving to himself he was "good" to his clients and to his children. Consequently, his efforts were directed toward proving she was "bad." She helped him along by behaving in ways that proved him "right" by her being "bad" in whatever situation they happened to be. They were so beautifully locked in this relationship that nothing else was considered. They seemed to love being hateful to each other, resisting any possible efforts to change. How could each define himself or herself otherwise if they divorced? Without the other, no self-definition, even in extreme terms (good-bad) would be present. Apparently, it was better to be defined according to such extremes than not to be defined at all. Each one needed the other to define himself.

Be careful then of either-or talk. It is extremely destructive to use because it does not fit all of the variations of human behavior. Another example of either-or talk that derives from either-or thinking is the separation of mates according to "I" and "you." Instead of "us" and "we," each of us tends to use "you" to talk about the mate and at the same time avoid talking about oneself. All of the energies are bound in finding faults in the partner. Hence the pronoun "you" becomes one of the most destructive terms there is, and the "I" is used only to show how good "I" am compared to "you."

How Do Marriages Become Troubled?

By now each of you should have become aware of hurtful patterns of communication:

1) "You" instead of "I", "it," or "we."
2) "Either-or" instead of "How many choices do we have?"
3) "Always-never" instead of "I seem to do this whenever I . . . etc."
4) "It's your fault," "It's my fault," instead of: "Given such and such an issue, what can we do to make it better?"
5) "I know what you are thinking (feeling, etc.)," instead of "I only know what I feel, hear, or see."
6) "I did it because of you" instead of "I did it because it makes me proud, it makes me feel good, or excited to do it."
7) "Yes" instead of "Maybe, let's talk about it."
8) "No" instead of "I am not sure, let's see what it means."
9) "I know what you think" instead of "I am not sure about what you said. Did I hear you saying . . .?"
10) "I know you said it" instead of "Let me check with you. Did you say that . . .?"

As you read these examples, what did you become aware of? Can you see how the solutions considered in each example are less hurtful, less limited, and less destructive?

The marriage with choices needs not be enmeshed in this kind of thinking, or, to put it another way: to change for the better a great many helpful choices are available to most of us. Unfortunately, many of us become unable to see them in the heat of battle and under the weight of trouble.

5
considering changes

Change is a tricky business. Most of us think of change as being outside ourselves, both physically and otherwise. Most likely, people who see change as something happening on the outside of themselves meet and marry partners who see the world in the same way. If this is the case, then both partners are locked in a deadly battle; each expects and wants the other to change. Neither is willing or able to see himself as needing to change to make it easier for themselves and the marriage.

The only type of change we are considering here and will be considering from this point is change *inside* of one's self—the hardest type of change possible. In fact, it is so hard that some of us prefer to be called "criminals" or even "kooks" or "crazy" and for society to take responsibility for our actions rather than taking charge of our own lives.

Choices and Change

In the heat of the battle, in the depth of our pain, hurt, and worry, it becomes very hard to see and consider choices. You may feel cornered, in a rut without any way out. In some serious cases, suicide or separation seem appealing ways of escape. How easy it may be to part and go separate ways. How easy it is to forego responsibilities and chores. How easy it is to avoid trouble by not confronting it. If and when we are in a rut, choices left to us are few and far between. Either-or solutions are all we have left. Either we divorce or we stay

Considering Changes

married; either we live or we die; either we have a marriage or we do not. At this point it is hard to consider creative, helpful choices for ourselves, our marriage, and our family. It is at this very point that various choices need to be considered. You have choices. Consider *some* of them.

Change by Chance

Choice 1: Keep your marriage as it is, that is, leave it to chance, fate, luck, or magic for the marriage to improve by itself. Here you are taking the chance that it will get better without any responsibility from either one of you to make it better. If you do nothing, your marriage will get better. How does this choice sound to you? Usually, if we keep things the same and do nothing, the chances of the marriage getting worse or better may be 50–50. One of you, the one who wants change for the better, may be betting it will get worse. The other one, who denies trouble and has an investment in keeping things as they are, the same, will bet that it will get better. However, (s)he will not lift a finger to see that it will. A lot of marriages are based on this hope: If you do nothing, things will get better and you can always put all the responsibility on your mate for the fact that it is not improving.

Change by Distance

Choice 2: Let us "split," either separate, desert, or divorce. This way, all of our troubles will be over. As long as the other mate is responsible for the trouble in your marriage, it follows that if you "split" all your troubles will be over. Right? Well, let us think about this choice a little more carefully: Sarah and Jerry decided to separate. They were miserable living together. Jerry moved to a small efficiency apartment and started living the life of the swinging bachelor. Back to the good old single days. No chores, no daily responsibilities, no putting up with temper tantrums, doctor bills, taking the children to school, etc., etc. Besides the financial strain that this arrangement brought, after all (Sarah wanted and needed to stay in the same house), Jerry found that he was thinking more of Sarah than he had. Although he tried, he could not become seriously interested in all the young girls available (readily?) in the apartment complex, and now he was spending more time with the children than he had ever done before.

On the basis of their temporary separation, Jerry and Sarah concluded that while they were miserable together, they were also miserable apart. They could not make it with *or* without each other. Yet the only other choice they considered was to give in and accept the marriage as they *both* made it—terrible. No other creative choices or solutions seemed available to them. Another variation of the same choice is deciding to divorce and to seek a lawyer, as we shall discuss in the next chapter.

Change by Choice

Choice 3: Either one of the first two choices has the same outcome; the marriage remains the same. Both partners are unchanged; how can their relationship change as well? Both choices are based on the idea that change should take place *outside* ourselves. Therefore, as long as we expect change on this basis, change will not come to us. The choice considered here deals with change taking place in *both* partners. Change of this kind, *inside* of us, can take place in many and mysterious ways. Some of us change on the basis of confrontation. Some of us change on the basis of conflict present both inside *and* outside of us. Some of us would like to believe that we change by chance and not by choice. Unfortunately, this last possibility leaves out personal responsibility for change. If there is no personal responsibility in change, there is no change.

Our marriage will not change unless we both desire it and recognize our helplessness to do anything constructive about it without our partner's help. Change starts in our recognition of helplessness in ourselves. We cannot change the world (although we may try), we cannot change our mate (and we may try). We can only change ourselves (which is very hard), while changing others is impossible.

Change by Commitment

For change to take place, both partners need to be committed to that goal so that their energies can be invested in change and not in keeping the marriage the same. Therefore, each partner needs to make a conscious, open, and direct statement concerning wanting to change. The deeds need to go with the words. Each partner needs to be very clear as to how each is going to change. In fact, they should be so clear about how they are going to change that they may want to put it down in writing to avoid confusion, forgetting, distortions, and misunderstandings.

Change by Communication

Change can and does take place between marriage partners if and when they care enough about themselves and each other to want to talk over any issue confronting them. Wanting to change a relationship means getting in touch, becoming aware, and expressing how the relationship is hurting and affecting one's self. This awareness of hurt, discomfort, and concern needs to be communicated to the partner without blame, accusation, or recrimination. Most of us find it very hard to obtain this goal. Some of us have trouble becoming aware of our discomfort. Some of us are unable to express such feelings in a helpful (rather than hurtful) way to our partner.

Ideally, communication means telling someone we care about and who seems to care for us how we feel without making that person responsible for our feelings. All of us are individually responsible for how we feel and how we behave. Unfortunately, oftentimes marriage becomes a boobytrap that allows us to dump this responsibility on our partner. Basically, communication means taking personal responsibility for our lives, our feelings, thoughts, and behavior without making others responsible for them.

Babs and Jim came to us after seeing many other professional helpers. For hour after hour they expressed their deep inability to take responsibility for their own actions by making their partner the culprit. The logic of such behavior is not only self-destructive but also irrational. As best we can figure out, it goes something like this: "Since my parents were cruel, I can be cruel too." or "Since you behave like a so-and-so, that means that I also can behave like a so-and-so," or "I behave like a so-and-so because you behave like a so-and-so."

As incredible as this logic may seem on the written page, it is nevertheless the logic of many of us who are unable to separate our own self from the self of our mate. Consequently, we become unable to take responsibility for our actions or to set clear limits to our own behavior and to the behavior we will accept from those we care about, especially our mate. As a result of our inability to take responsibility for our actions (as we shall discuss further in various parts of this book), we crystal-ball, mind-read, and speak for our mate. We "know" how (s)he feels, thinks, and acts and, therefore, we speak for them. This destructive practice has at least three distinctive hurtful outcomes: (a) it does not allow our partner to speak for himself; (b) it takes away from our having to speak for ourselves; and (c) it takes the whole marriage away from dealing with more relevant issues. Hence, the extreme importance to talk about oneself, using the pronoun "I" or "it" or "we" instead of the hurtful "you." Show us how often the pronoun "you" is used in a marriage and we will tell you how troubled that marriage is.

Change for Whose Sake?

If you want to change your mate or your children, forget it. It will not work. Change can only take place inside of us or it will not be change. You can force others to do what you want. You can blackmail, bribe, cajole, coax, and plead with them. However, that will not be change. Or, if there is an apparent change, it may well be short-lived. To last, change needs to come from the *inside* of us, not from the outside.

Change, therefore, can only happen *for your own sake* and no one else's. If you change for the better, those around you will benefit by it. Of course, what you think is "for the better" may be for yourself and not for them. If they are used to your saying "yes" all the time and doing everything they want, clearly they will think you are out of your mind if one day you tell them that you will not play servant any more! What is change to you may be a threat to others.

Change Is a Two-Way Street

Just because your family is accustomed to how things are does not mean you should accept the situation and be part of any effort to keep it as it is—unchanged. Do you accept life as it is given to you, or do you make any effort to improve it? If you do not put forth any effort to improve it, why should anyone else? You can change your life if you change yourself. However, we want change mostly when and while we are hurting. If there is not hurt there is very little desire to change. Why should we change if everything or almost everything looks rosy?

Change is not easy and it does not come when things go well. If you want to feel better about yourself and those you love, what you may be experiencing now may mean that a change is necessary. However, change does not take place in a vacuum; it could involve your mate having to change, too.

Only Strong People Can Change

The only way we know we can use the label of "strong" and "weak" is in relationship to change. In our experience, strong people ask for help when they hurt and strong people can change. Some people feel so weak that they are unable to ask for help to change. (We will clarify in future chapters what we mean by "asking for help.")

Change will not take place in your marriage unless you (1) quit expecting that your mate (and the world?) change for your convenience; (2) get in touch with the helplessness that derives from this realization; (3) accept the position that you cannot change anybody else but yourself; and (4) accept that changing oneself is the most difficult of all tasks.

How many couples we have seen who were not able to agree on having a better marriage! Why? Because each of them was unable to realize this simple fact, that *in order for the marriage to change for the better, each of us needs to change for the better.* Many of us are unable to see this point and expect change to take place in others.

Is your marriage worth fixing? Whether your marriage is worth improving and working on is a completely personal choice that each person needs to make. Now you have to decide whether whatever is troubling your marriage will repair itself or whether it will get worse if you wait. Again, this decision is entirely yours. Each of you needs to decide whether you can make it on your own together, whether you want to make it without each other, whether you want to make it *worse,* or whether you want to make it *better.*

Change by Confrontation

If your partner cannot share with you a need for change or seems unaware of any reasons for change, then your marriage is in serious trouble. If you are able to finish a problem-solving discussion without ending it in a heated argument, you are in good shape; you may not need help. However, if after opening up your concern about changing you find yourselves further apart, this is a good sign that your marriage is troubled.

If you can confront issues calmly, face them, solve them, sit down without bad feelings and arrange at least one hour a week for discussion of the issues we all face every day of our lives, and if after these discussions you both feel better, masterful, and proud of yourselves, you do not need to be concerned about how troubled your marriage is. If it works for you and you like who you are and what you have, make the best of it. You may not need to read this book any further. However, if you think that marriages should be without conflict, you may have to reconsider. A certain degree of conflict is really necessary in marriage—any marriage—as long as the conflict is used to confront underlying issues and to change and improve the marriage. Conflict can be used to build the marriage or it can be used to destroy it. It depends on how you two are able to deal with it.

Joyce and Ron have made a pact that every time one is irritated by whatever the other is doing, he or she should tell the other right away. If either one forgets and does not bring it up within twenty-four hours, it cannot be brought up again and used against the other.

Jesse and Mary, on the other hand, without talking about it, have agreed not to bring up anything that irritates them. Instead, they have tacitly agreed (they have never dealt with this issue openly or directly) not to say anything that bothers them when it happens. Therefore, each of them secretly and unknown to the other maintains a list of "wrongs" that the other one has supposedly committed. This list is brought out only when they have a fight or an argument. They use their secret list of past hurts to hurl at each other gleefully and angrily. Which of these two couples do you think will have a chance to make it in their marriage? Why? Which of these couples does your marriage resemble?

Considering Changes

Very likely one of you is apparently more unhappy than the other about your marriage. The other may deny or belittle any problem or trouble. Yet, the one who denies and belittles will show his or her unhappiness in other ways. For instance, (s)he may have trouble at work, or may have trouble with friendships, or with the children. In other words, while one of you may be able to *talk* about your unhappiness, the other may show it through actions rather than through words. Even then, any confrontation of unhappiness may be taken as a personal threat, insult, and offense.

Your discussion at this point may go something like this:

FM (First Mate): I have been reading this book about making our marriage better and . . .

SM (Second Mate): What's wrong with our marriage? Why do you always need to look at the bad side of everything?

FM: Well, as I just was . . .

SM: If you stayed home more often instead of . . .

FM: But I mean . . .

SM: I know what you mean! You are telling me I am no damn good.

FM: No, I'm not. I just thought it would be a good idea if we . . .

SM: What do you mean "we"? Count me out. . . . What did you want, the honeymoon to go on and on and on?

FM: Well, you know what I mean. We talk very little with each other and we don't seem to spend time to make our marriage better.

SM: What do you expect anyway? You must be looking at TV too much. . . .

FM: Well, I thought it would be a nice idea if . . .

SM: You are full of nice ideas. In the meantime I've got a million things to do and you want to work on our marriage! You have got to be crazy!

Obviously, this kind of "discussion" could go on and on, and it does in countless households across this country, sometimes kinder, but more often than not, harsher than the illustration here.

Clearly, in discussions like this, one of the partners has some investment in keeping things as they are. Awareness of tension is denied, conflicts and hurts are belittled, and confrontations are avoided. Therefore, no matter how you may approach the matter of working for a better marriage, you will get a negative reaction, resistance, rejection, rebuffs, anger, or sadness. Any attempt to change the system already established is bound to produce waves.

The main way you will get through the initial explosion or reaction is to stick determinedly to your position. If your goal to change is worthwhile and positive, why should it produce such a reaction? Let us put it this way: Look at a pond that is muddy and dirty. If you throw a stone in it, you will not make the pond any clearer, but you will get some ripples. If the pond is yours, you will need the help of others, including your mate, to clear it up. However, if you do not know how to clear that pond, you may need to consult an expert. It will not clear itself.

If the matter is important to you and is serious enough to be talked about, go about it in a serious fashion. For instance, one way (and by no means the only or right way) would be to make an appointment with your mate: "There is something important I need to talk about. When can we get together to do it?" As soon as you open up the discussion in this way, you can be sure that your mate will try to draw out what the matter is and get you into a discussion right then and there. You need to stick to your guns. Avoid being drawn into a quick and dirty arrangement. You could say something like this: "I know you are curious about what it is, but I think it is important for us to wait until the time we set. How is tomorrow night?" As soon as you set a time, whatever it is, you can bet that the line will be, "What's wrong with right now?" Again, this is a way for you to lose control of the situation, if you lose the time and place, you lose control as well. Stick to your opening statement by saying something to the effect that "Tonight we are both rushed. We have to finish supper and you said something about a TV show you wanted to see. Furthermore, one of us has to drive Lisa to basketball practice. I doubt whether it would be a good time. Is tomorrow night a good time or do you have a better time, with no interferences from the children or TV?"

Suppose you are both finally settled down and are able to talk about your marriage at a time and place where no interference is

Considering Changes 65

present. What then? You need to make your wishes and intentions clear to your mate without putting him or her down. You could say something like this: "You know I have thought a lot about our marriage. There have been a lot of good times and a lot of not so good times. I would like to make our marriage better. However, I feel that I cannot do it by myself. I need help. Can you help me?"

At this point, very likely your mate will be upset, perhaps even shout or scream, trying to get you into an argument rather than into a problem-solving discussion. If such a possibility seems clear, back away from it by saying: "I am sorry but I cannot give you an argument about it. I would like to change myself to make our marriage better." Such a statement very likely would provoke a question to the effect of: "What's wrong with our marriage?" If this is a relevant question, be prepared to answer in full without raising your voice (if you can). You could say: "I am glad you asked. Let me tell you what I think is not working in our marriage. I feel we are in a rut, we avoid each other, we argue a lot, and when we do get toeether, we can't enjoy life, etc., etc."

Remember: Discussion rather than argument. Can you solve problems without getting angry? Can you stick to your agreements after you have made them? Can you put into action what each of you said you would do?

The goal of this meeting is to get your mate to work for a change *together.* If you cannot get together on this point and your mate does not want to work with you, you have a problem.

Change by Contract

If you want to really save money and avoid getting involved with anyone outside of yourselves, then you may consider contracting. What is it? Well, by now you may have forgotten it, but if and when you were married in a religious ceremony, you may remember the minister, rabbi, or priest saying something about "taking each other for better or for worse . . ." and other words that at that time may have not had any meaning for you.

Perhaps it may be necessary to look at your marriage contract. Not the one that someone else read over you. We mean your own marriage contract. Something so important that you both may want to write it down.

To begin with, each of you may start your own list of what you want from each other. After each of you has written that list, make an appointment (yes, an appointment; things like this are too important to deal with by chance) to go over your individual lists. Exchange lists and read them carefully. Then, take another piece of paper, and as you talk and become aware of each other's needs and wants, start writing up a Master Marriage Contract in which you both list what is most important to you in rank order. For instance, some of you may want to consider first how you feel about fidelity. Others may feel that truthfulness is important, etc. Avoid using abstract, general terms, and try to use very concrete words.

As you write down this master contract, think about what each of you needs to do in order to follow and honor what you are writing. If there are points there that you do not feel sure about, say so. Do not allow anything to be written down unless at least one of you feels strongly about it.

You need to make this contract as specific and detailed as you possibly can. You can break it up according to topics (Us, Our Marriage, Our Sex Life, Our Children, Our In-Laws, Our Budget, etc.), and you can even write down what each of you is willing to do to accomplish what you want.

After you have finished, do two things: On the top write "First Draft." On the bottom sign your names. At this point, set up an appointment for a week later, at a time when there will be the least distraction from the children, phone, neighbors, etc. During this week mull over some or all of the points you have made and consider what changes you will want to make that would be agreeable to both of you. It should be clear by now that all the points you have made on this master contract should be *agreeable to both of you.* If one of you cannot subscribe to a specific point, discuss it until you both are satisfied with it. If one of you cannot feel good about a point, erase it or put it aside for further discussion. After you have gone over your first draft and made all the changes each of you wants, make two copies of this revision, one copy for each of you to keep and to mull over and not misplace.

At this point, we would suggest that you keep up your weekly meetings to talk over whatever points in the contract need further attention from both of you.

Now comes the joker. Contracting is the best test of how your marriage is working out. If you have been able to reach agreement on various points in the contract, and if, more importantly, you have been able to honor and follow this contract without undue hassles, then you may be on the road to recovery. If you both are happy with the contract and following it has changed and improved your lives and your marriage, then you may not need to go any further for help.

However, if writing this contract has become just one more hassle, and you have not been able to achieve agreement over many of the points, then watch out. You may be in trouble. Furthermore, you may have succeeded in writing up a more or less satisfactory contract. However, if either one of you has had trouble following it, then, again, watch out. You may still be in trouble!

We are suggesting, therefore, that you use some very clear steps to judge how your marriage is working out and whether you need external help with your marriage. In a previous chapter, we suggested that if reading this book was a hassle between you two, then maybe you *were* in trouble. Now, we are suggesting that if contracting did not work for you, then you may need help from the outside. Contracting is one way of improving marriages. If it did not work for you, you may need to try something else.

Separating or Deserting

Other choices, like separating or even deserting, are available to you. Why not take some time out, why not move out of the house and into an apartment and kind of cool it for a few weeks or months? Even better, why not chuck it all, leave the house, the children, the job, and go away to start afresh somewhere else? These are tempting possibilities, but is there anything constructive in them? Separating for the sake of separating without either one of you changing is just a postponement and a delay of any other decision you may want to make. Of course, you will have peace and quiet for a while, but what will that peace and quiet get you, if neither one is learning anything new about himself or herself and the marriage? Is this separation another of the many magic distractions that you have used in your marriage? Start counting what it will cost to maintain two separate households. Start becoming aware of how lonesome you (at least one of you) will be. Start considering what you will do differently that you were not doing while you were together. If you can come up with new plans or new projects different from the past, if you are so inventive and imaginative, you may want to think about why you are so creative away from each other. Why is it that you cannot be creative together?

Many, many couples cannot be constructive about their marriage because they are bound to defeat each other. In the process of defeating the other, they are not aware that these defeats are really harmful to themselves. Neither one is proud of how he is behaving but each is unable to change himself. In fact, more often than not, divorce, or separating, is another one of the many changes made outside of oneself. Since many couples are hell-bent to change their external environment through divorce and separation, we will need to consider if changes can be internal to the marriage rather than external. It means changing from a "You should be different" to a "Both of us should be different (and better) for this marriage to survive!" How can we go from trying to change the other one to changing ourselves? Think how easy it is to put the blame on the other one, use all the information we have gathered on the other's faults in court, and then walk away free! You can be free of your mate. You can become free of your marriage. You may even become free of your children if you want that bad enough (by deserting and other irresponsible acts). However, we venture to say that you are stuck with yourself. How can you live better with yourself so that you can make a constructive decision on whether to stay married?

6
asking for help

Change for the better in marriage is an emotional issue that taxes all of our resources: emotional, mental, and, of course, economic. You invest money in repairing your car; why not invest money and effort in changing your marriage when all else has failed?

Change Is Asking for Help

We cannot change unless we (1) admit we need help; (2) seek the help we need; and (3) use the help available to us to improve ourselves. Trying to change without external help is like expecting your dishwasher to repair itself when it is out of order or your car to fix itself when it is leaking and making strange noises. Asking for help is the first requirement of change.

Believing that one's marriage will mend itself by itself is one of the most self-defeating ideas about marriage. In fact, it hides a form of thinking that goes something like this: "If it cannot fix itself, by itself, 'chuck it'! If we cannot stay happily married, let us split." What would happen if you traded in your car every time it made some strange noise? Well, no matter how rich you may be, you will trade a lot of cars! Can you see how this kind of thinking produces so many divorces? Many otherwise sane, intelligent, competent, and educated couples think like this.

Considering a Lawyer

One way of asking for help is to see a lawyer. Millions of couples do it, why not you? Eventually, you may have to take that step. A few lawyers may suggest a cooling off period, or suggest a counselor, or even attempt to help both of you with your marital problems. Unfortunately, our laws and our legal structure are designed so that if you really want a divorce, the lawyer is ethically bound to help you get one. Most lawyers will treat you as adults who have made their decision to get a divorce. However, before you make this decision, consider the following points.

It costs more to destroy a marriage than to build one. The legal fees plus the usual economic chaos of divorce will cost more, or at least as much, as it would cost for both of you to work for a better marriage. Talk to a lawyer, get his figures, and put them all together. After you have done this, ask yourselves whether you could use this amount of money to work toward a better marriage.

The lawyer will do the work, and you will not learn anything. Clearly, the lawyers (by now you should have one for each of you) will work for you, saving you a great many hassles and potential struggles. As a result of his work, you will be spared a great many arguments, mistakes, and aggravations. You learn absolutely nothing new about yourself and your marriage. Evidence of this is seen in the many people who seek help after the divorce, when they no longer have a culprit, their mate, to blame and thereby avoid looking at their own inner depression and hurt. If you want to learn something about yourself and your marriage, why not do it before the divorce?

If you do not learn anything about yourself and your marriage, how can you be sure that you will not make the same mistakes in a second marriage? Divorce is an investment to destroy without any learning. Possibly more constructive choices could be considered to help you avoid it!

The lawyer will have an investment in seeing your marriage ended. His living may depend on it. No wonder we now face a wave of books and self-help manuals on Easy Ways to Divorce, Creative Divorcing, and counselors specially "trained" to pick up the pieces *after* the

Asking for Help

divorce. But if there is money and effort to be spent, why not use them on the marriage?

Have you thought about the fact that in this country we have laws to break up marriages, but we do not have laws to preserve them? Are you aware that there are more lawyers willing and able to take your money and break up your marriage than there are trained professional helpers to help you work on your marriage? The lawyer works for you. He gets you the divorce. What else do you want for your money? Thus, after the process is finished, you are not only poorer in money, but even more importantly, you will be poorer in knowledge about yourself and your marriage. The lawyer will help keep you the way you like yourself, only without the benefit of a mate who (heaven forbid) attempted to mar the image of your perfection. So relieved, you can go on being exactly the same as you were before the divorce. Now you should be on top of the world. Are you? If you are, see how long you can stay there.

If the thought of a lawyer turns you off, you may be open to a more constructive solution. You have waited long enough, and your previous attempts have failed to work. Your marriage is in a rut, and you want more for yourself and your family. If this is the case, ask for help! Why should you? Consider the following: (a) asking for help is cheaper (in energy and money) than not asking for help; (b) asking for help may allow you to change your life and make it better; (c) if worse comes to worst, you may learn something about yourself; and (d) what you learn about yourself may allow you to behave in more positive ways than you have done before.

Asking for Help Is Cheaper

In talking about costs, we need to separate money from feelings. There is no price for feelings. How we feel is what we are. Therefore, when we say that asking for help is cheaper, we need to explain "cheaper than what?" If the choice you are now facing is whether or not to ask for help, let us consider both your feelings, for which there is no price and no need to pay a lawyer.

Hiring a lawyer, paying court expenses, and doing whatever else is necessary to obtain a physical divorce is using money to destroy a relationship. Yet, even though you may get a legal divorce that ensures physical separation, you need to consider whether each of you will be emotionally disentangled from each other and whether each of you will be able to survive the loss of the other. A great many people, for instance, seek and get help *after* their divorces to heal the wounds caused by divorce.

Start adding up what it would cost to break up your marriage (and your friendly lawyer will be very helpful in giving you an idea of the expenses) and what it would cost to work on your marriage by asking for help. Of course, there are intangible costs that have no dollar value. How much is your happiness worth in money? Do you have a system to translate personal satisfaction into dollars and cents? How about your feelings of hurt and the way you are wasting your energy running in circles? Can you put a dollar sign on these factors?

The wear and tear on your emotions, as most people who have gone through divorce proceedings know, is tremendous. The emotional cost is great and the repair work afterwards will not restore the marriage. It may make it easier for you to face life again by yourself to consider meeting other potential mates, and possibly to avoid making the same mistakes you have made in the past.

The cost of legal proceedings involving lawyers on both sides and court expenses can climb into the thousands of dollars. Furthermore, your financial situation will never be the same with separate households, alimony, lack of insurance coverage for medical expenses, etc.

If you choose to do nothing and go on as you are now, it may not cost any money. However, your feelings will take a beating because, by refusing change, both of you are essentially saying that the feelings of one of you, the one who hurts and who is strong enough to admit it, do not count. Not asking for help will, therefore, mean a denial of these feelings. How long can either one of you live with this denial? Who will pay the price of your unhappiness? You? Your mate? Your children? Does anyone need to pay such a price? After all, denial of how you feel means denial of you. You do not count. If you care about yourself, do not let yourself down, do not let such a denial take place. If your marriage is important, is it worth investing in?

Making a Better Marriage Through Help

Help may not make a marriage better. In fact, it may make it worse. In order for help to work, it needs to be based on changes in both partners, not just one. If both of you change for the better, your marriage may change for the better. If both of you change for the worse, so will your marriage.

Why should you consider help? Well, for openers, asking for help with your problems may be the most constructive, positive thing you may do in your life. Ask yourself this question: What do I have to lose? Are you afraid of looking at yourself? What do you think you will find? Is looking at yourself so painful that you are willing to sacrifice your marriage and your family? To be sure, there are millions of individuals who have done and are doing just that. If you like what you see in the mirror every morning and want to keep seeing the same face, by all means you should not seek help.

Learning About Oneself

Of course, learning about yourself is the last thing you want! If you are perfect, why should you learn anything new about yourself? It is all your partner's fault; therefore, what else is new? You know your problems well. You have read all the books there are to read. What else can you learn? You read Ann Landers every day, and you can see that it is not your fault. Why should you change? These and many other questions will be raised because asking for help is the beginning of change. Up to the present, you may have been "spinning your wheels" in attempting to change your partner, your job, and your children (not to mention in-laws).

Why should you ask for help? After all, asking for help may mean to admit to personal hurt and error. Asking for help implies assuming personal responsibility. Asking for help is done by adults. Asking for help is a mature, responsible act. It implies taking risks, wanting change in your life. It means commitment to one's self and to one's marriage. More importantly, asking for help means caring. If you do not care about yourself and your marriage, asking for help is not an option, since it is clear that you do not want change. If your investment is in keeping things as they are and especially in keeping yourself the same, do not invest in help. Asking for help is a caring act born of strength. If things are not bad enough for you, wait until they get worse. Asking for help is a positive act that few can perform. After all, there are many more people asking for divorces than there are people working to avoid divorces! By denying personal responsibility and claiming great strength and independence, you are avoiding change. In fact, change may be so frightening that no attempt is made to obtain change!

Thus, asking for help is one way of avoiding divorce. This book is concerned with helping you get help with your marriage and, if possible, avoid divorce. By asking for help for your marriage, you may be doing yourself a favor because you may have started one of the most exciting parts of your life, and you may be about to use and exploit all of the best that is in you and in your marriage.

Once you have made the decision to ask for help, put your energies into getting the best help you can get and getting the most from the help you get. This book will attempt to help you in the process. It should help you avoid divorce, and it should make for a more positive marriage.

Avoiding a divorce does not mean settling for a "lousy" marriage and giving up what is important to you. Avoiding a divorce implies a positive, caring act of asking for help and, once help is gotten, making sure that you use it for the enhancement of yourself and your marriage.

Should We or Shouldn't We?

Both of you may be sitting on the fence, waiting for something to come along which may improve your marriage. While waiting, you are marking time. The checklist in chapter 4 may help you decide whether you should seek help. It may have given you some guidelines; however, let us make clear that the decision to seek help is a strictly personal one. There are people who will seek professional help because of bad dreams or fantasies. There are people who would never dream of asking for help no matter what. If you want help bad enough, you will look for it no matter what the objective aspects of the situation. In matters of this kind, the decision cannot be based solely on the objective situation.

How you feel when you get up in the morning matters more than

Asking for Help

any objective reasons. If you feel miserable and rotten in your marriage, ask for help. If your marriage is not working out *for you,* ask for help. If both of you are determined to defeat each other and cancel each other out in every decision that comes up, ask for help. If you argue continuously, unless you like it, ask for help. If you are both growing bored, mad, and sad in your marriage, ask for help. If neither one of you can laugh and enjoy life any more, ask for help. If your children are becoming symptom-bearers, that is, acting up, acting out, underachieving in school, etc., ask for help.

If your children are hurting, it means that your marriage is hurting, too. If your marriage is hurting, each of you is also hurting. If you care for yourselves and each other, ask for help. If you do not feel proud of yourself and the way you act, ask for help. If you do not feel good about yourself and your marriage, ask for help.

Of course, you can wait until things get worse, until one of you becomes a confirmed alcoholic, or starts running around, or becomes an inveterate gambler, or acts in other ways that would be destructive to the marriage. Perhaps you both need a violent shock to show you how much you need help. If you want to delay and postpone, you can. However, consider the following: By then you both may be so far apart that no marriage can be rebuilt; or one of you or one of your children may have become so disturbed or disturbing that no professional helper can be found to help any or all of you; or the cost of putting together all the pieces may be so high that by then you cannot afford it.

The argument, of course, deals with prevention versus cure. You know the old proverb about an ounce of prevention being worth a pound of cure. It works in your marriage as well. Whatever help you can get to prevent trouble will be worth it. Of course, you need to be careful about where and when to get this help. We will explore these possibilities in the next chapters.

The Best Cue

Finally, since almost everything at this point in your marriage may be a hassle, very likely reading this book will be a hassle too! One of you, the one who is making waves demanding change, may want the mate to read it. Consequently, there may be an argument about this book and the points made here. The issue, then, of who should be reading this book and the arguments that may come out of reading or not reading it will give both of you an indication of how troubled and disturbed your marriage may be. Neither one of you can support anything that the other proposes. Does this sound familiar? Then it is clear that this book and its recommendations will be belittled, criticized, laughed at, and rejected.

If this is the case, try to keep your discussion to the basic issues: (1) Do you want change in your marriage? (2) If you want change, do you want change for the better or for the worse? (3) If you want change for the worse, that is, expensive and destructive changes, you do not need this book or its recommendations. (4) If, on the other hand, both of you are interested in changes in your lives and in your marriage, you may consider some of the suggestions made here. (5) Do not be sidetracked by irrelevant or distracting arguments; stick to the issue of change for the better and how it can be achieved. (6) If you can get change for the better without outside help, congratulations. (7) If you cannot or will not change for the better on your own, you may consider some of the suggestions made in the next chapters.

Your mate may still choose: (1) not to admit that (s)he is unhappy; (2) to deny that something is not working either for himself or for the marriage; or (3) to separate himself from your happiness. (S)he may refuse to help you in your search for a better life. If this is the case, the possible consequences may be made clear to him or her in terms of: (1) costs, both in emotions and money, and (2) threat to the marriage. Why should one stay in a marriage where no sharing of unhappiness and of solutions is possible? Marriage is for us to share most of our unhappiness, since everybody else, from the bartender to the hairdresser, will be glad to share our happiness. If your mate is not concerned about sharing your unhappiness as well as your happiness, what good is your marriage? Can a marriage exist where there is no care? Only you can answer these questions.

7
fighting change: arguments against help

There are many ways to fight or avoid change. Some ways are obvious and blatant. Other ways are not. Some people prefer a divorce to changing themselves. Other people would like to stay in the marriage, no matter how troubled, without changing. In this and the next chapter, we want to consider some of the ways many of us use to either fight or avoid change. Of course, such a list may not be exhaustive. However, by now the reader should have been able to see the many ploys and plots we all use to avoid change.

One way to avoid change is to attack the personal and professional qualities and qualifications of professional helpers. Another way is to equate professional helpers with craziness.

"I Am Not Crazy"

"Only crazy people go to see shrinks. I am not crazy; therefore, I do not need to see a shrink." Or, "Shrinks are for nuts, and it takes a nut to see a shrink."

Perhaps you can see the many errors in logic made in those few sentences. In the first place, no one needs to be "crazy" to seek professional help. As a matter of fact, it takes pretty healthy people to seek and get professional help. The argument that only seriously troubled people seek help is a form of denial usually used by the mate who has an investment in keeping things as they are. He who does not want change does not want help. Since seeking help is perhaps the first constructive change you may have considered in your marriage, the possibility of change is opposed as are other issues in the marriage.

Another common excuse, in addition to the "craziness" argument, is that everybody (and especially your partner) should see a professional helper, but, God forbid, not you. You are strong, well-liked at work, successful in your own way, fun at parties. Why in the world should you seek help? If it were not for your incompetent partner (or child or in-laws or a particular behavior that bugs you), you would be okay.

After all, change is threatening. It means behaving differently. It means learning something about oneself and, even worse, it may mean changing oneself! "If I'm okay, why should I need any help?" We know of many mental health professionals whose marriages went on the rocks because one of the mates, learned and all-knowing, refused to seek help with the other mate who was desperately asking for it. Apparently, these individuals must have been fearful of admitting their helplessness and giving up their smug position of knowing it all. It takes a lot of guts to ask for help. Perhaps these people were too weak to admit needing help!

"My Mate Needs Help, I Don't"

"(S)he needs to see somebody; I don't." This second argument to avoid asking for help as a couple is a well-known ploy to keep things as they are and avoid change in oneself and in the marriage. Clearly, you two did not marry at random. One of you may even look "sicker" than the other, or better yet, may play the "sick" role while the other plays the "healthy" role. This is just an instance of the either-or thinking we mentioned earlier. In a marriage there are not "sick" and "healthy" people, but there are individuals who hurt and who hurt each other. And because they hurt, they are proving they care for each other. Strangers we do not care about cannot hurt us as those who are close to us can.

Give up the fiction that one of you is better off than the other. That fiction will not work, but will drive you further apart. It is another instance of one-upmanship that derives from the possibility that one of you may be locked in a downmanship. No one's position in any marriage is reached without the consent and oftentimes the help of the other one. Whatever position each of you has reached in

Fighting Change: Arguments Against Help

your marriage is due to the actions of both of you. Both mates have allowed or even encouraged one another until you both have reached a position neither of you likes. However, you both entered the marriage. You both made it into a lousy marriage. You both can get out of it if you want to, or you both can make it better.

"Help Is Costly, Time Consuming, and Too Distant"

"Anybody who pays that much money to get help must be crazy to begin with." You are right; it may be expensive. However, it will not cost, we venture to say, any more than buying a new car and less than going to a lawyer for a divorce. Is your marriage less important than a new car? Why are you willing (and able) to invest in a car and not in your marriage? Clearly, the one of you who resists change will use any excuse to avoid change. "We cannot afford it" is usually a statement made even before costs and returns are considered and compared. If this statement is made without knowledge of the facts and fees, it is clearly based on the unwillingness of that mate to seek change. If you can afford a surgeon for a broken arm, a car to get around with, or a lawyer to destroy a marriage, you can afford getting help for yourselves and your marriage. However, if you enjoy being miserable and making the other one miserable, no one can take that away from you.

Another variation of the same theme is time: "I don't have the time." "I'm too busy." "You mean we need to go there once a week. For how long?" You might consider the time devoted to activities that do nothing for the marriage or that may even be destructive to it. Lacking time is the ultimate put-down of a marriage. It implies that the job, children, community activities, or what have you are all more important than the marital relationship. This may well be the time to reconsider one's priorities in life.

In some locations, distance may become a factor: "It's too far to go." "It's so many miles ... what, with the gasoline shortage and costs being what they are, it is impossible for us to go." Considering the time we Americans spend on the road, both in public and private transportation, for our myriad activities, distance may well be the most irrelevant of excuses.

"Shrinks Are Crazy, Too"

"Shrinks are either crazy to do what they do, or they have marital troubles, just like us. How can they help us?" Again, this is another version of an incomplete argument based in part, a small part, on the fact that professional helpers are human beings; and all human beings are vulnerable, hence all professional helpers are vulnerable. There are professional helpers and professional helpers. As we will discuss at length in another chapter, you need to clarify which kind of professional helper you need and which ones you can do without.

Of course, professional helpers have problems in living just like anyone else. Of course, they are prone to fail, just like anyone else. They are not perfect and if the burden of change in your marriage is put on them, your marriage is destined to fail. Hopefully, the professional helper may have learned to take care of himself and his marriage to the point that he will be able to help you. However, once they have helped you sort out your feelings and your thinking, the responsibility and the will to change yourself and your marriage in ways that will pay off is yours, not theirs.

"How Good Are Shrinks?"

"Mr. and Mrs. Johns went to see Dr. X and one of them ended up at the state hospital. What good are shrinks?" Oftentimes, especially in this kind of extreme case, help has been avoided until one family member breaks down. In other words, getting professional help was avoided until the last possible moment, when there was little that could be done except hospitalization. Any professional helper spends a great deal of time seeing and talking with helpless individuals, couples, and families who have avoided and postponed getting help while they were most able to profit by it. Eventually, one family member, the one to whom the family has assigned the role of the "sick" one, breaks down and is hospitalized. He is usually the scapegoat selected by the couple or the family as the symptom carrier and reliever of their own tensions and conflicts. In our experience, the one who is identified as the patient is frequently much less "crazy" than the rest of the

Fighting Change: Arguments Against Help

family. Unfortunately, though, the pressure to be sick is too strong to overcome.

Another argument goes: "Remember the so and so's? They went to a shrink for years. Look what happened to them! They split and each of them is dating someone else!" This kind of argument is another example of using external props to avoid looking at oneself. It does not matter what the so and so's did with their lives. There are plenty of couples who "mess themselves up." Because they were unable to profit from help, does that mean you have to be as destructive and helpless as they were? Therefore, this excuse is not enough to avoid seeking help. Take it for what it is—another way of fighting change.

"There Are Worse Marriages than Ours"

There is another more subtle way to avoid change and not seek help. It goes something like this: "Our marriage is lousy, but there are worse marriages than ours." "Those couples do not ask for help. Why should we?" Again, note how, in this argument, attention is given to circumstances outside and not to those inside the marriage. Certainly there are thousands of troubled marriages. Of course, there are thieves, criminals, and many unhappy, hurt people in this world. Does their presence and existence justify our not living in ways that are rewarding to us and to our children? Does the unhappiness of others justify our own unhappiness? Must we live miserable lives because others do? Clearly, the responsibility to live our lives to the fullest is ours and ours alone.

"My Parents Made It All Right"

Another argument given to avoid change and seeking help goes something like this: "My parents had trouble too, but they made it all right." Sometimes the hidden implications here are "I made it all right in spite of the lousy marriage my parents had." "What was okay for my parents should be okay for me." Hence, lack of change in others, whether relatives, friends, or neighbors, is used to justify one's investment in keeping things as they are. Furthermore, in this argument, there is an implicit admission of unhappiness in one's family of origin and apathy to do anything about the unhappiness. It is a denial as well as an admission of unhappiness. Like many of the arguments used in this chapter, it is contradictory. It does not stand up to logic or to facts.

In spite of all these ploys, the final issue that needs to be decided is: Do you want change for the better in your lives and your marriage? You both have the final answer to this question. Yet, you may still sit on the fence of doubt, indecision, and postponement. In fact, to avoid change, you may employ more subtle and indirect ploys than those considered in this chapter. These ploys will be considered in the next chapter.

8
avoiding change: shortcuts won't help!

You want to avoid a divorce, and you are committed to change in your life? If that is what you want for sure, then there are some pitfalls you should know about. Chances are that the strategies that are here called "pitfalls" you have already tried. If they worked for you, don't knock them. Consider yourself lucky that you have been able to obtain change in your life with a minimum of effort. Indeed, what are here listed as dangers may have been somebody's life-long salvation! How can one really judge? The ultimate judgment, of course, lies in the results. These pitfalls are the most common, the most human, the most obvious ways to seek help. There is nothing wrong with any of them if they work. Here, we will consider ways we all use to seek relief from pain and a way out of our rut. We will consider what will *not* work most of the time in most cases.

After all, why avoid divorce? Why should anyone put energy in avoiding a divorce? What is the positive aspect of avoiding a divorce? It is working for a better marriage. If you do not know how to work for a better marriage, the best you can do is ask for help, as was argued in the preceding chapter. In the process of asking for help, however, you may fall into some misconceptions that may not work well for your marriage. Pitfalls can be divided into two classes, one consisting of methods, the other of people. Oftentimes, the methods and the people can overlap.

Advice Is Cheap

To begin with, you are hurting if you want help. To find help, you will turn to anybody willing to give it to you. If you want immediate, quick, cheap and easy help, you will find it. Of course, this is a good way of avoiding change; that is, trying to get quick, easy advice. In other words, if you get advice when you are asking for help, you are not getting help. You are getting what you are asking for: a quick, magic way out. There are many kinds of advice, and some of it is thoughtful, helpful, and given with care and consideration. However, there is also advice for quick, immediate actions that is of doubtful value. It may come in the form of "Do this, do that" or "Don't do this, don't do that." Impulsive actions have little room in marriage, especially if these actions are hurtful to someone. If the intent of these quick actions is (a) to take revenge; (b) to get even; (c) to hurt; (d) to manipulate someone (either you, your mate, your children, your parents, or your in-laws); or (e) to emotionally blackmail, bribe, or browbeat, forget it. All of these are hurtful ways of behaving, and chances are you will not enjoy using them, much less be proud of them.

There are many people who will give either advice or quasi-magic prescriptions and suggestions. They can be easily identified as: (a) well-intentioned friends; (b) loving relatives; (c) irresponsible charlatans and quacks; and (e) inappropriate professionals. "The road to hell is paved with good intentions," and there is nothing as destructive as a person without experience and knowledge but with lots of good intentions. One of the most destructive intentions of certain individuals is to be helpful.

Beware of emotional band-aids. They cannot work miracle cures. Changing a marriage and avoiding divorce is not a process to be achieved in two or three quick, easy lessons. Think of all the time and effort that both you and your mate have put into making a mess of your lives and then consider whether any quick, easy effort will cause a turnabout. Only an experienced professional will know what is involved in obtaining meaningful change. However, let us consider why anyone who is not qualified should help you and why you would want their help.

Avoiding Change: Shortcuts Won't Help!

Admitting to needing help, getting in touch with our basic helplessness, is very, very hard. Before admitting to the seriousness of the situation, should you check it out with people you trust? Maybe they will suggest shortcuts that will help you avoid seeking professional help. You will find yourselves seeking these shortcuts and you are entitled to seek them. However, consider the possibility that these shortcuts may be other ways to avoid change.

Asking Well-Intentioned Friends

Well-intentioned friends may be very willing to give you advice and tell you what to do. However, the advice will be based on incomplete information since the friend will very likely have only your view of what is going on in your marriage. And if your view is so clear-sighted and undistorted by emotion, confusion, and faulty thinking, then why would you need advice in the first place?

Another drawback of seeking advice from a friend is that of putting yourself in the position of being the ignorant child before the all-knowing parent. The parent will tell the child what to do and then the child has no alternatives left. He either follows the advice or, if he does not, he is essentially disregarding the importance of the parent. An example of this is the wife who confides to a friend that her husband is being unfaithful. The common, quick and easy advice, loaded with righteous indignation, is to "throw the bum out." This kind of advice is either to be followed or not followed and leaves out a multitude of other options that could be explored. Neither acting or not acting on this advice will lead to a happier life. And if the advice is ignored, the friend may feel used and offended. Essentially, what we are trying to say is that advice robs us of those decision-making abilities that as adults are ours and ours alone. When we ask others to live our lives we are giving up the responsibility of living our lives ourselves.

Loving Relatives

Among the many sources of advice are loving relatives, those who really care for us and who hurt when we hurt. Their commitment is to help us avoid hurting. As a result, they rush in with band-aids —quick advice that may help us in handling an immediate, minor crisis but does not last long and does not change anything basic. Quick advice is the best way of avoiding permanent changes. If changes are to take place in your marriage, they will be the product of prolonged, planned, and serious hard work on both your parts. Quick advice is a short cut that avoids all of that effort. Without effort there cannot be any significant change. Quick advice avoids commitment, promises a great deal, delivers very little. Avoid it if you can.

Seeking advice from loving relatives may also have the additional hazard that they may interpret the trouble you are in as a reflection on them and their influence on you. After all, they are okay and they did the best they could for you, so why are you in trouble? Why is it that what worked for them is not working for you? What worked for them was in a different time, a different place, and in different circumstances. In the present situation, they may feel as helpless as you.

Frequently, it is very difficult for loving relatives, because of the very fact that they are loving, not to take sides. They will be very able to see the justice of your position and to understand the burdens under which you are struggling, but will fail to see the equally heavy burden your mate is carrying. One-sided views seldom will lead to helpful advice. It is usually advice which will result in one partner winning at the other's expense.

Charlatans

One measure of a professional helper is his practice of avoiding giving quick advice, making snap judgments, and jumping to unreasoned conclusions. The charlatan usually has a magic plan, a quick gimmick, an optimistic outlook, a sure-fire thing. He will be unclear about his credentials, his qualifications, his experience, his memberships in professional associations, and his link to other professional helpers in the community or in the county.

The increasing number of people in need has resulted in an increasing number of charlatans, especially in the marriage counseling field where little legislation and control exists, except in a few states. The marriage counseling field is one of the few areas where charlatans can bypass laws, legislation, and legitimate requirements. You will spot the charlatan by the quickness of his decisions, his name dropping, and his trying to stay clear of local institutions and other professionals. No matter what the problem is, he can handle it. There will be no careful assessment as to whether further referral to other professionals is required. A qualified professional knows his limits and will not attempt to take care of all possible problems that come his way.

A word of caution is also in order on the number of sex therapy clinics appearing all over the country. This is a field in which quackery abounds.

Inappropriate Professionals

Although there are many qualified and competent mental health workers who possess impressive credentials and experience, you need to remember that the majority of these professionals were trained in individual rather than marital therapy. Working with marriages is a specialty of its own, and being trained and experienced in working with individuals is not enough to work with couples. Hence the first question you need to ask is: Is the helper willing to see us as a couple? If the answer is no or maybe, you may want to look for someone who clearly tells you that he was trained and has experience in working with couples.

There are also a number of persons from unrelated professions who have drifted, through natural bent, into marriage counseling. There are a number of attorneys in family practice, who in the course of giving legal advice on wills, deeds, contracts, divorces, etc., have found themselves in effect doing marriage counseling. Some few, liking this work, have sought additional professional training and have qualified themselves to follow this turn in their careers. Others would do well to refer clients to those who are qualified professionals.

9
religion and change: its uses and abuses

Since change is a personal matter, there is no way to consider it without including how we feel about our religion. What we believe in this area is part of our selves. Hence, it is impossible to separate self and change from religion.

Is Religion Necessary?

Even without religious affiliation and formal membership, both mates will need to decide on their values and priorities in life. They may choose not to call these values and priorities "religion." Yet, both mates will need to come to terms with, confront, and consider what is important to each of them and to both. Similarities and differences between themselves can be sources of personal and mutual enhancement or can be abused to debase oneself and the marriage. Religion may be one of these sources. It can unite the partners or it can divide them. How we use or abuse religion is up to each of us.

We want to deal with both positive and negative aspects of religion. As far as we are concerned, the positive uses of religion deal with change in ourselves for the better. The negative uses of religion deal mostly with avoiding change for the better and keeping things as they are in ourselves.

Positive Uses of Religion: Enhancement

Religion may be used to enhance our lives and the lives of those we love. Such an enhancement or change for the better is achieved in a variety of ways.

Religion and Change: Its Uses and Abuses

To Achieve Comfort in Oneself

Religion can be a source of much-needed comfort in our daily lives. It is a realm of experience different from anything else we experience in our workaday lives. It is not the technology made up of objects, TVs, appliances, cars, houses, etc., that surround us all. It is not competition that makes us all try to strive to be above our neighbors. It is not part of the rush-rush routine that envelopes us all. It is part of our most intimate self that deals with the most important issues of our lives, the meaning of us on earth and the meaning of us at death and beyond. It is an acknowledgement of our impotence, of our realization that there are areas in our lives which we can not control, the ultimate being death. It forces us to consider how we will live the lives we have. Rejection or acceptance of religion in one fashion or another implies something about how each of us defines his or her own self.

To Give Meaning to Oneself

Religion then, in whatever form or fashion we choose to practice it, deals with our values, what is important or not important to us. Hence, it is important in the marriage, since who we are and how each of us chooses to live affects our relationships with others, especially our mates.

To Obtain Changes in One's Life

Religion can be used to enhance our marriage or to debase it. If we use religion to live our lives and to define ourselves positively, very likely it will be a positive aspect of our marriage.

To Assume Personal Responsibility

If our religious beliefs and practices allow us to see ourselves clearly, to see our errors and mistakes without putting the responsibility on our mate, and if religion allows us to draw clear lines on what behavior we will put up with in ourselves and our mates, then religion can be helpful. Some of the issues that relate to such practices will be considered in greater detail in a future chapter on getting hold of one's self.

To Get Appropriate Help

Religion can be used to get appropriate help. Our minister, priest, or rabbi can be either a direct source of help, if he is trained in this area, or he can be a good source of referral to those who are.

Some clergy are well prepared to help couples in trouble, while others are not. You both will need to judge how far and how much your clergyman can do to help you with your marriage. If he can and does help, consider yourselves lucky. If he cannot help you, at the very least he should be able to direct you toward more appropriate sources of help.

Negative Uses of Religion: Debasement

If religion is to be used to debase the human condition, we do not need that kind of religion. There are enough areas of our lives that may lead toward such a debasement. However, we should make one point clear. Most religions in and by themselves do not debase our lives. We ourselves choose to abuse our religion to debase ourselves. It is what we make out of our religion that matters.

Religion as a Magic Escape

Often we may use religion to escape the pain and hurt of our lives and we would like for our religion to act as a soother of our ills. We expect religion to heal everything in our lives in unclear and undefined ways. If and when such miracles do not happen (is the marriage getting any better?), we make religion the culprit for our failures.

Expecting Too Much from Religion

To expect religion to take care of our apathy, helplessness, and our failure to take charge of our lives will not work. It is too much to expect. For instance, if you expect your religion to heal your marriage without each of you taking personal responsibility, you will wait in vain.

To Avoid Personal Responsibility

Religion can be used to assume a stance of righteousness and blame everybody else, especially one's mate, for a troubled marriage. Under these conditions, religion is used as a weapon.

Another just as destructive use of religion is the assumption of martyrdom, or sainthood. The individual feels so bad about himself and life that he enjoys setting himself up to be put down, to be taken advantage of, and debased. The underlying feelings of worthlessness may be so strong that being "crucified" becomes a source of pleasure and satisfaction. These individuals would like to think that the more they suffer on earth the more they will be rewarded in heaven. Consequently, they set themselves up to be miserable and make anybody else miserable around them. These individuals play the parts of superpatriots described in chapter 4 or those of band-aid givers.

Religion as Appearance

Very often we see in our office individuals who attend services regularly and give the appearance of being quite religious. Yet we sometimes wonder if their faith helps them to behave positively and creatively in their lives. Without realizing it, we can become overdependent upon religious observance for reasons which are sometimes in conflict with our faith itself. We can neglect the true spirit of religious faith out of an intensely felt need to protect ourselves from the pain of personal hurts. In this situation, religion is sometimes used as a way of shielding ourselves from the truth. It becomes a matter of appearance. Yet, we cannot and will not assume the position of judges and jurors. Clearly we cannot tell anyone what religion may mean to them. However, if religion becomes only a matter of appearance or is used as a means to debase oneself or one's marriage, it is important to put it in perspective. In chapter 4 we touched lightly on membership and activities as part of the checklist to judge the degree of trouble in a marriage. Especially when mates differ in religious background, each may use his religion to club the other. We both recognize the personal significance of our particular religious background and the pride each of us has in being raised in that background. If each of us respects the religious background and beliefs of the other, such affirmation can bring about an enhancement of the self and of the marriage.

SECTION 3
doing something positive for a change

10
seeking help in groups

The possibilities considered in this chapter are more likely to help working or trouble-free (?) and mildly troubled marriages. In chapters 11 and 12 we shall consider possibilities for moderately and seriously troubled marriages.

In a location where there would not be many choices available, there are still some possibilities present. We will suggest a few, from the least to the most expensive. Either way, regardless of cost, you will need to put time aside to work on your marriage. Therefore, you need to commit yourselves to taking time out of other activities (including work) to assure that your marriage receives the attention it deserves. We will suggest a variety of alternatives, choices, and possibilities open to you. None of these are mutually exclusive. You can follow one or all of them. Whatever the extent of your commitment to change, we can assure you that your marriage will not suffer from an excess of helpful alternatives. In fact, our personal feelings are that any marriage can stand the help of a variety of approaches. This variety will give you the opportunity of widening your awareness and experience by meeting different people with sometimes completely different approaches. The wider the range of choices open to both of you, the greater the possibility of your finding what you need specifically. If possible, give yourselves the chance to become involved in as many marriage-related activities as there are realistically available in your community.

Self-Help Groups

Self-help groups consist of people who help themselves without the intervention of professional helpers. Examples of such groups are: (a) Alcoholics Anonymous, a group that had done more for alcoholics than any known scientific approach; (b) groups, similar to Alcoholics Anonymous in scope and methods, which have mushroomed across the country, such as Gamblers Anonymous, Neurotics Anonymous, Recover, Weight Watchers, etc. Single parents have their own group known as Parents Without Partners. We are just beginning to explore the usefulness of self-help groups with adolescents, children, and mixed groups. These groups have an enormous, untapped potential to take over many of the functions that in the past were assumed by the extended family. Our mobility has made it difficult for many of us to depend, use, and rely upon our larger families. It follows that we need to learn to rely upon our friends, our neighbors, and interested semi-professionals.

One of the major issues in many of these self-help groups is the leadership, since a great deal of the group's success will depend on the nature and extent of the examples from a few leading individuals.

Parent Effectiveness Training (PET)

This program was developed by Thomas Gordon of Pasadena, California. It is available in book form and can be ordered at your bookstore. On reading the book, you could apply some of its principles to your marriage and see if they work. If you need further instruction, you can attend one of the PET workshops often held in some of the major cities. It is recommended for laymen and lay instructors. Basically, this approach is based on the method of active listening, direct expression of one's own feelings, and give and take based on feelings. Once you learn some of its methods and apply them successfully to your marriage, the same principles could be applied to your family, your neighbors and friends, and your work. Similar approaches are William Glasser's *Reality Therapy* and Albert Ellis's *Rational-Emotive Therapy.*

Transactional Analysis (TA)

This approach is based on the ideas of the late Eric Berne, whose writings are available almost anywhere. Like PET, this approach has gained a great deal of popular favor, and instructors and workshops are available in most large centers in America.

The major characteristic of this approach is becoming aware of three different parts we play with our spouses in marriage: as Parents, demanding that the other behave the way we want him to behave; as Children, refusing to follow what we are told to do; and as Adults, behaving according to what each situation requires for resolution.

Both PET and TA may be useful to your marriage. However, if your marriage is seriously troubled, do not expect for these approaches to be cure-alls. From a financial viewpoint, they will cost less than individual counseling or therapy because they are given in large classes or groups. Avail yourselves of either or both and try to apply these approaches to your marriage. However, if they do not work for your marriage, you may need more professional help. TA must not be confused with TM (Transcendental Meditation), a helpful form of self-relaxation and control.

Church

The church can be a tremendous source of strength as long as it is not used as a magic cure. When we are sick, we may pray for health, but we also seek the help of a doctor and follow a healthful regimen.

In the church we can find, if we look for them, members who will be willing and sometimes able to help us. Unfortunately, there is also the issue of privacy. It is difficult to open up to people who are close to you but who may not respect your privacy. There is always the fear that your troubles may become public knowledge or the subject of common gossip. To protect yourselves from these unfortunate possibilities, you need to be selective of whom you approach and how you approach them. Clearly the issue of confidentiality, to assure you that the information you disclose will be respected, needs to be considered seriously.

Another possibility would consist of forming marriage-study groups across church denominations, asking for couples from different churches to participate. If handled properly, many of these groups can be successful. There is strength in numbers so that a variety of couples, sharing the common bond of needing help, can become a source of possible solutions for some of your problems.

You could put out feelers among the church members. Is any couple interested in a marriage study group? Are there couples willing to commit themselves for better marriage through work rather than through wishful thinking? Explore this possibility; you may be surprised by what you find. If your efforts come to nought, at least you know that this is a dead end. Be careful in judging others because they do not share your interest. Just because they are not willing or able to come together with you does not make them less worthy members of your congregation. Explore, but do not demand. Keep your energies for exploring other possibilities.

Neighborhood

Spread the word that you are interested in a marriage study group. Call friends, neighbors, politicians, clubs, and civic organizations. Announce your intention to start such a group. Offer your house for the first meeting or if your house is not adequate for such a meeting, find a room in the Sunday school building, in the school, or in a club for such a purpose. Collect names and telephone numbers of couples who may be interested in pursuing the same course of action. Proclaim for anyone to hear the importance of marriage and of your desire not only to preserve your marriage but to make it better.

Structured Programs

In the last few years we have seen the rise of many self-help books trying to help couples deal with their marriage, so some of these materials could be used as a basis for discussion in self-help groups. Depending on the nature of your group, you will find some useful materials available at relatively minor cost.

Many of these programs need to be in the hands of mature and experienced individuals. Some leaders in your community could be encouraged to obtain them and to get the necessary experience that goes with their administration. There are at least three different types of groups that could be set up, depending on the nature and severity of their problems. The first group could deal with marriage enrichment for couples whose marriages are working well but who want more out of their marriages. The second group could be made up of couples who do need help in their marriages above and beyond enrichment. Both partners need to learn how to get along, how to reach decisions, how to express themselves, and how to enjoy being married rather than to suffer through marriage.

The third group could be composed of couples concerned about their responsibilities as parents who would inevitably deal with their marriages. We have not yet found a couple who had trouble as parents who could not use help as partners. How can we be parents if we cannot be partners? How can we learn to be parents if we have not learned how to be a husband and a wife?

Clearly most of these programs, even with how-to-do manuals following a cookbook approach, need leaders. It would be infinitely better if these leaders were couples or husband-wife teams with supervised experience.

Remember now that you will not be able to get these programs yourselves, because someone needs to be responsible in working with you in using them. However, you may suggest that people involved in helping you may look at them and see whether they can be useful in helping you. A professional helper should be supervising or helping whoever is helping you. At this time, they cannot be used by laymen without any training or supervision. Eventually, though, these programs could be used by interested, mature man-woman teams of volunteers or semi-professionals under supervision from a professional. In this way, costs could be drastically reduced and more couples could be helped.

Marriage Retreats

There have been for some time now movements (Marriage Encounter, Marriage Retreats) that encourage the couple to go away from their usual everyday setting to an isolated place where they will meet with other couples in trouble. These marriage retreats usually take place on weekends. When they are available, week-long programs for couples to work on their marriages during their vacation or other available time when the breadwinner can take leave would be the most valuable.

Many of these retreats are run by experienced individuals who have seen many, many couples. However, such retreats should not be taken as substitutes for more prolonged, day-by-day, week-by-week efforts. They are more in the form of a marriage "cure." They could be used in addition to seeing professional helpers or coupled with other self-help groups and structured programs. They are not intended to take the place and to be used instead of programs that extend over time.

Directory of National Marriage Enrichment Organizations
(Provided by the Association of Couples for Marriage Enrichment
[ACME])

The marriage enrichment movement, as it is now being called, is developing a wide variety of programs across North America. Some of these are organized locally, some regionally, some nationally.

To make a beginning in charting this new development in our culture, we have selected only those organizations which appear to be providing, on a national scale, specific programs in marriage enrichment for married couples. The programs vary somewhat in nature and in scope, but the most common forms are the weekend retreat and the growth group that meets at regular intervals.

We do not consider this list to be complete, and it will obviously have to be extended in the future. For the time being, we are confining it to a group of organizations that are already in touch with each other, and some of which have already sent representatives to national meetings where information has been shared and future policies and plans discussed.

Ten of these organizations have expressed a wish to be linked together for ongoing consultation and cooperation, in the newly-formed Council of Affiliated Marriage Enrichment Organizations (CAMEO), with ACME serving as convener.

Association of Couples for Marriage Enrichment, Inc. (ACME), 459 South Church Street, P. O. Box 10596, Winston-Salem, N.C. 27108, telephone 919–724–1526. Paul and LaDonna Hopkins, Executive Directors. ACME was established in July, 1973, as an organization of couples "to work for better marriages, beginning with our own." Its purposes are (1) to support and help each other in seeking growth and enrichment in our own marriages, (2) to promote and support effective community services to foster successful marriages, and (3) to improve public acceptance and understanding of marriage as a relationship capable of fostering personal growth and mutual fulfillment. Membership is open to married couples who agree with ACME's purposes and goals. Associate Membership is open to individuals. Dues are $15 a year. Members receive regular newsletters and may purchase books and cassettes at discount prices. ACME covers North America (U.S.A. and Canada), has national officers, state and provincial representatives, and contact couples in local communities. Local chapters organize weekend retreats, growth groups, marriage communication courses, lectures, conferences. Publication—David and Vera Mace, *We Can Have Better Marriages—If We Really Want Them* (Abingdon Press).

The Christian Church (Disciples of Christ), Marriage Communication Labs, 222 S. Downey Avenue, P. O. Box 1986, Indianapolis, Ind. 46206, telephone 317-353-1491, extension 469. The co-directors of the program are Frank and Loraine Pitman. Begun in 1972, this is part of the program of the Department of Christian Education of the Division of Homeland Ministries and covers the U.S. and Canada. Weekend marriage enrichment experiences are conducted in a retreat setting, and some weekly sessions and other variations have been used locally. The national office works primarily with regional offices to sponsor training and oversee the total program. Over eighty couples have been trained as leaders, and several hundred couples have participated in labs. Emphasis is given first to developing communication skills, then to applying these skills with specific aspects of marriage such as conflict, sexuality, values, and roles.

Christian Family Movement, 1655 Jackson Boulevard, Chicago, Ill. 60612, telephone 312-829-6101. National President Couple: Ray and Dorothy Maldoon. Established June, 1949, became ecumenical in 1968. Members in forty states in the U.S., Canada, and in forty-five other countries. Purpose is to promote and sustain Christian family life. CFM is primarily a married couples' movement made up of small groups (usually five to six couples plus clergy) meeting in homes biweekly, using programs prepared nationally, with emphasis on action. Membership is open to couples and families interested in Christian marriage and family development through a formation-through-action program.

Friends General Conference (Quakers)—Marriage Enrichment Task Force, 1520 Race Street, Philadelphia, Pa. 19102, telephone 215-107-1965. Chairperson: Shirley Bechill, 185 Pineview, Alma, Mich., 48801. Marriage Enrichment Retreat Program was started as pilot project in 1969, now operates through yearly and monthly meetings in the U.S.A. and Canada. Marriage enrichment retreats are offered in accordance with opportunity and need, conducted by trained leader couples. Two pamphlets, "Marriage as Vocation" and "Marriage Enrichment Retreats," have been published.

Couples Communication Program, Interpersonal Communication Programs, Inc., 2001 Riverside Avenue, Minneapolis, Minn. 55454, telephone 612-338-4276. President: Sherod Miller. Inquiries to Ms. Debbie Mandrigues. Program developed from research since 1969 at the University of Minnesota Family Study Center. It offers an educational program designed to improve communication skills between couples. Programs are offered by trained and certified instructors to groups of five to seven couples. Program available in the U.S.A., Canada, and Germany. Over 500 instructors already trained, and 2,000 courses conducted. Publications: *MCCP Handbook; Alive and Aware: Improving Communication in Relationships.*

National Council of Churches—Office of Family Ministries, 475 Riverside Drive, Room 711, New York, N.Y. 10027. While the Council conducts no direct programs of its own, it acts as a clearinghouse for information and a cooperative training center for its 31 member denominations.

National Marriage Encounter, 955 Lake Drive, St. Paul, Minn. 55120. National Executive Secretary Team—Jerry and Marilyn Sexton and Father Tom Hill. The Marriage Encounter program was started in Spain around 1958 by Brother Gabriel Calvo, and was introduced into the United States in 1967 through the Christian Family Movement. Marriage Encounter presently is active in 36 states and has been taken up by the U.S. Military in its overseas installations. Although based on Catholic tradition, it is open to couples of all faiths, and presently a number of groups are operating which are primarily Jewish or Protestant. The stated purpose of the Marriage Encounter is "to discover God's plan in marriage through the enrichment of the marital relationship and growth of the partners as individuals and as a unified couple." The program consists in a weekend experience of deepening communication between husband and wife, using the techniques of "personal reflection" and "conjugal dialogue." The weekend is conducted by a clergyman and two or three trained couples, although the actual "encounter" is experienced between the husband and wife privately. The individual Marriage Encounter groups around the country devise their own follow-up programs, although these are fairly standard. A national magazine, AGAPE, is published on a monthly basis, and an annual National Marriage Encounter Conference is conducted. These are among the services offered by the National Office, which, rather than being a policy-setting apparatus, is primarily a resource center and a national representative for the Marriage Encounter movement in the United States.

Moravian Church, North—Marriage Enrichment Program, Board of Educational Ministries, 5 West Market Street, Bethlehem, Pa. 18018, telephone 215-867-0593. Contact person: G. William Sheek. This program was begun in 1972, and covers the northern United States and Canada. Its purpose is to motivate couples to become involved in a variety of marriage enrichment experiences, and to design and facilitate couple growth events ranging from four-day lab experiences to weekly study groups. More than 100 couples have participated in marriage labs, and a much greater number in other sharing and educational experiences.

National YMCA—Family Communication Skills Center, 350 Sharon Park Drive, A-23, Menlo Park, Calif. 94025, telephone 415-854-3884. Director: Winifred J. Colton. This Center was established in July, 1970, in accordance with YMCA national policy for enhancing relationships and improving communication. Uses a variety of program models to help couples, parents, and families with problems before they become crises. Models are: Positive Parenting, Family Communication Program, Positive Partners, and Peoplemaking through Family Communication. Other models are in the process of development. Professional leaders and materials are available to schools, churches, YMCAs, mental health organizations, etc. The Center has already organized 51 workshops, and trained 900 staff and volunteer leaders from 370 cities representing 33 states and one Canadian province.

Reformed Church in America, Marriage Enrichment Program, Office of Family Life, Western Regional Center, Orange City, Iowa 51041, telephone 712-737-4958. Director: Delbert J. Vander Haar. The Marriage Enrichment Program began in 1970 as part of a policy of Office of Family Life to encourage local congregations to give high priority to meeting family needs. Primary focus of the Marriage Enrichment Program has been for pastors and wives, more recently extended to the laity. Approximately 200 pastors and wives have participated, and a network of 14 family life associates and wives are trained to provide leadership. Currently, a premarriage model for engaged couples is being developed.

Southern Baptist Convention, Family Ministries Section, 127 Ninth Ave. North, Nashville, Tenn. 37234. Joe Hinkle. No report.

The United Church of Canada—National Support Group for Couples, 85 St. Clair Avenue, Toronto, Ont., M4T 1M8, Canada. Directors: Fritz Schmidt and Robin Smith.

United Methodist Church—Marriage Communication Labs, Board of Discipleship, P. O. Box 840, Nashville, Tenn. 37202, telephone 615-327-2700. Directors: Leon and Antoinette Smith. After several years of working with married couples, a national training program was developed in 1966. Couples from twelve major denominations have been trained and several have established their own programs. This model has been shared with couples throughout the U.S., Puerto Rico, and nine other countries. More than 450 leader couples, trained through MCL, work with an estimated 10,000 couples each year. Typically a MCL is a 48-hour experience involving ten couples plus two participatory leader couples. The time is equally divided between (1) total community with experiential input on some specific marital topic by the leaders, and (2) two nonstructured small groups (five couples plus one leader couple). Emphasis is on communication in marriage. Other marital issues dealt with are chosen in response to the expressed needs of the couples. These might include creative conflict, sexual enrichment, identity-intimacy, goal setting, etc.

United Presbyterian Church—National Presbyterian Mariners, Box 1270, League City, Texas 77573. Executive Secretaries: Barbara and Ed Looney. The Mariners provide a couple organization, whose purposes are to establish Christian homes, to offer Christian service and outreach, and to provide Christian fellowship. All offices are held jointly by couples. An annual family convention and several family vacation weeks are organized. Emphasis is mainly on Christian nurture within the church, but endeavors in the field of marriage enrichment are now being developed in the form of marriage enrichment weekends, using the services of ministers and other trained leaders where available. No leadership training in marriage enrichment has yet been undertaken.

The enrichment programs and organizations we have just discussed have the quality of being limited in time, that is, once a week for six weeks, one weekend, etc., and large in number, anywhere from three to thirty couples, depending on the program used. You can get these programs through your clergy if you can find enough other couples in your church or neighborhood to make it worthwhile for someone to come into your church.

Enrichment Is Not Counseling or Therapy

Help comes in many and unexpected ways. We ourselves have experienced many different types of professional help. Yet, the help that was most meaningful to us came from a friend, Dan McDougald. He is an attorney who gives most of his time to developing emotional maturity instruction or semantic reconditioning programs for the rehabilitation of prison inmates and criminals. If you do not give yourself a chance to find these ways it will be impossible to find out which method works best for you. We tried as many as we could to get something from the many viewpoints, methods, and leaders available in the United States.

The bewildering range of possibilities is staggering. Yet we do not know what does and does not work for each couple. Reading books, including this one, will not change your life or make your marriage better. We are rather skeptical that books alone can or do change anybody.

Enrichment consists of a variety of exercises, lessons, tasks, homework requirements, questions, and issues which are presented to you in a prearranged way. They may or may not be helpful to you depending on how seriously troubled your marriage is. If your marriage is mildly troubled, you could benefit by enrichment programs. They should not hurt even if your marriage is moderately troubled, but you may need further help, like counseling. Counseling, or therapy, on the other hand, is much less structured than enrichment. Counseling usually takes place over a longer period. The duration depends on a variety of factors, including how both of you are using the help available.

Therapy is somewhat different from counseling in the sense of being more extended in time and lasting up to a few years. It is clearly the most expensive, but sometimes cheapest, form of help you can get. The cost undertaken depends on how much you value your life and your marriage. (We shall refer to both marital counselors and therapists as helpers.)

In an enrichment program, the enricher asks you to answer some specific questions, perform some specific tasks (look each other in the eyes, talk to each other, etc.). Before enrichment begins, you will most likely have agreed on how long or how often you will meet (usually not more than one weekend or no more than 6 to 12 hours), and how much it will cost you. This kind of specific information is very hard to get in counseling or therapy, which may vary from a few weeks to years and which may cost a few hundred dollars to thousands.

Of course, there are as many varieties of enrichment programs and people offering those programs as there are varieties of people and marriages. The enrichment program you may find may work out well for the majority of marriages. However, you may not like whoever is offering it. Allow yourselves to experience more than one enrichment program and definitely more than one enricher.

Most enrichment programs take place in groups, usually in groups of couples or parents. On the other hand, most of the programs developed by the authors are designed to apply to individual couples or families. One way of distinguishing between enrichment programs and counseling or psychotherapy is on the basis of structure. By structure is meant the length of time, the form of each meeting, and the cost. What will take place during each hour in an enrichment program is already predetermined by the program itself, while what will take place in one hour of counseling or therapy is determined mostly by the couple themselves in terms of the issues they want to bring up to the counselor or therapist.

Another way to distinguish between enrichment and counseling or therapy is in terms of generality. Most enrichment programs apply to general issues and problems that are universal to all of us in most marriages. Counseling and therapy, on the other hand, are more specific. They are tailored to the specific and unique needs of the couple seeking help.

A third way of distinguishing between enrichment and counseling or therapy is on the basis of preventive versus curative treatment. Most enrichment programs are preventive, while counseling and therapy are treatment for moderately and seriously troubled marriages. This distinction does not mean that both cannot be used. For instance, some enrichment programs under certain conditions could be used in addition to or in conjunction with counseling and therapy.

One of the greatest values of enrichment programs is preventive. The other important value is the enhancement of a marriage or family that is already working well. These programs can and should be used mainly with ideal and adequate marriages. Enrichment programs could be used with some selected mildly troubled marriages. With moderately or seriously troubled marriages, enrichment programs could be used *only* in addition to counseling or therapy.

In terms of their preventive use, it is clear that enrichment programs (including those developed by the authors) can be used by a variety of well-functioning and working marriages. This, in fact, is the most important and relevant application of enrichment programs. There is a need to prevent trouble, and these programs on a large scale could help avoid a great many of the ills besetting our marriages and families in this country by making marriage and the family the center of our lives. "An ounce of prevention is worth a pound of cure."

Consequently, on the basis of everything that has been said thus far, it would seem that, in a very rough and ready fashion, we could match degrees of satisfaction and trouble in marriage (discussed in chapter 3) with methods of helping marriages:

TABLE II

Type of Marriage	Type of Help
Ideal Satisfaction	Nothing or enrichment programs or similar experience
Average Satisfaction	Enrichment programs, retreats, or similar experience
Mildly Troubled	Enrichment or counseling or both
Moderately Troubled	Counseling or therapy with additional enrichment or other helpful experiences
Seriously Troubled	Therapy with additional educational and enrichment experiences plus social and environmental changes

Remember that there are as many counselors and therapists as there are enrichment programs (perhaps even more). Do not be discouraged by what may seem a disconcerting or seemingly inconsistent variety. Look at this variety as representing all of the many choices available in a country such as ours. You as a consumer may find it hard to choose. Getting "stuck" with someone you do not like is just as dangerous as going from one helper to another. Being "stuck" does not mean you have no choices; on the other hand, skipping from one helper to another is another way of avoiding change. Somewhere in the middle of these two extreme there may be the best compromise for you, who are the only ones who can judge.

11
finding a helper

If you have followed some of the suggestions given in the previous chapter and found that they worked, it means that your marriage may have not been as troubled as you believed. However, if you have tried group and structured programs which did not change your marriage as much as you would have liked, it may mean that your marriage is in greater trouble than you thought. Consequently, if your marriage is in moderate or serious trouble, you may need to seek a helper or helpers who will be willing and able to see both of you over an extended period. Let us see how we can help you find a helper for both of you.

Community

In your community there are many organizations that may be of help. If listed in the yellow pages of your phone book, call the local mental health association. If your community is small, call the mental health association in your county. If you cannot find it in your county, call the mental health association in the larger community close to you. Explain what you want to do and see whether they can help you.

Locate by telephone the closest mental health clinic. Ask them whether they have any marriage-oriented counselors or therapists. Ask for a professional who may help you in this regard.

Outside the Community

If there are no mental health facilities in your community, call the local state hospital or regional mental health center. You do not need to be mentally ill to get help from the state hospital. Many of these facilities would much prefer to spend their resources to keep people and couples healthy on the outside rather than to admit them inside. Most have outpatient, walk-in clinics. They may not help you with a self-help group but they will help you with your marriage. They may have the only available mental health personnel in your part of the county, and their fees, if charged, are usually nominal. Use them as much as you can, and go of your own free will as a responsible citizen who wants help.

As we warned you in a previous chapter, seeking appropriate professional help is not easy. By "appropriate" we mean professional helpers who are trained and experienced in working with couples in trouble. The process of finding such helpers can be started by calling the local mental health association, the psychology department of a nearby college or university, the medical society, or by word of mouth. In this process you may get names from your minister, friends, your physician, or your child's school counselor. One of the best recommendations for an appropriate professional helper would be from a couple who has been helped by that helper. That means you should keep your ears open to your neighbors and friends about possible suggestions. Get as many names as you can. Try to get as much information from your source about the professional qualifications, personal orientation, and success of the helpers you are considering. In the process of selecting the best for yourself, keep in mind the following qualifications needed to help your marriage.

How to Go About It

Once you have compiled your list of possible sources of help, whether they are institutions (clinics, hospitals, churches) or individuals, check them out. Get on the phone and ask to talk either to the individual whose name you were given, or if you are calling an institution, ask for whoever is qualified and interested in working with couples.

Finding a Helper

Usually an institution screens and controls the professional qualifications of its staff, so that it is safer to call institutions first. It is in the private practice field that you need to be careful lest you fall in the hands of a charlatan or of inappropriate professional helpers.

Once you are able to reach your sources on the phone, ask them whether they work with marriages in trouble. Try to assess whether their practice is exclusively with couples (it gives you an idea of their commitment to, and specialization in, marriage). As you talk, try to get a feeling about how comfortable you feel talking to them. Of course you would not want to judge the competence of any professional helper merely on the basis of a short telephone call. What we are suggesting is that you pay attention to how they sound to you. Do you like the tone and sound of the voice? Is the voice that of an individual you would like to see and meet personally? Does it inspire trust and confidence in you? In addition to how they sound, what do they say? Does what they say make you feel good as you are talking to them? Or are you getting uptight as you listen and talk?

In addition to the professional and personal qualifications that you need to assess, there are two more qualifications that you need to check. Have the helpers dealt successfully with their own marriages? If they have not, why not? If they have not succeeded in their own marriages, how successful can they be in helping others? Your questions may raise some anger on the part of the helpers. After all, how can anyone question their marital qualifications? In fact, the more divorces and marriages they may have gone through the more qualified they may feel. Do not be concerned about their reactions. By putting them on the spot, you are checking on their level of maturity. The issue is not whether they are married or divorced, but whether they learned anything from that experience. After all, the experience of going through a divorce and a possible remarriage may have helped foster the helpers' maturity concerning marriage.

You will also want to know something about the helpers' family orientation. Are they miserable loners who feel qualified to work on marriages and families strictly on the basis of paper credentials? Are their credentials (titles, names, institutions, schools, hospitals, etc.) as important as their personal, marital, and family qualifications? Our personal, admittedly biased, answer to that question is definitely, yes.

On the other hand, we are sure that we will find many contrary arguments to this position. In the meantime, we will stick to our guns: to be maximally effective with troubled marriages, professional helpers need to be as personally, maritally, and familially qualified as possible, especially if their area of claimed specialization is marriage.

Credentials Versus Credibility

There are extremely well-qualified professionals who may be unable to make you trust them or feel trusted by them. Credentials in the helping field are not enough. It takes more than credentials to make a professional helper interested in working with couples in trouble. It takes personal concern and care on his part. It takes a level of emotional maturity that will shine through and that you will become aware of as you interview, even on the phone, each one of them. It would be helpful if you and your mate could afford the luxury of personally interviewing two or three professional helpers before deciding on which one you want. Unfortunately, more often than not, this will not be possible. Realistically, you will need to realize that professional helpers are like cars. They come in different sizes, colors, and above all, prices.

Seeking Perfection in the Helper

We do not, of course, want to suggest that you seek and find the perfect helpers. They do not exist. There are professionals with varying degrees of expertise, different personalities, different training, different experiences, and different orientations to the problems of marriage. Instead of seeking perfection, we suggest you find whomever you feel comfortable with who can help you in the long haul. For the short haul, use friends and relatives or family professionals whom you trust, like your clergy or your physician.

Not Finding It (Perfection)

If you strive for perfection in yourself, want it in your children, and wish for it in your parents, too, you really are in trouble. No matter what, anyone you meet will disappoint you, including the professional helper. Surely you will find flaws in his or her personality, approach, ideas, etc. The issue is not one of perfection but one of

Finding a Helper

workability. Can you both work together with that helper? What other options do you have? Can you find other helpers? In what kind of city or community do you live? That will determine how many choices you have available to you. Usually, the larger the city, the greater the range and type of professional helpers that will be available to you.

12

seeking private helpers

In the previous chapters we considered using various institutions which offer services at no fees or at nominal fees. In this chapter, we shall consider services for pay.

The variety of professional helpers in this country is staggering and confusing. Who should go to see whom, where, and at what price? Unfortunately, even with such a variety, we run into the whole range of communities, from those where you will not be able to find even one qualified helper to larger communities where choosing among many is a problem.

Referral Sources

There are three types of professionals who may not be able to help you directly with your marriage. However, they may tell you where to find help or often they will feel qualified to help you directly. If they do and they are helpful, fine. However, you may feel uncomfortable getting their help and it is important for your marriage to level with them, asking them to help you find the best possible source of help. These people are the clergy in your church or temple, your physician, or lawyer. All of these individuals, especially if they have been around your community for some time, will be glad to direct you toward possible sources of help. It is the nature of their work that makes them experienced in such matters. You are not the first couple to ask them and you will not be the last.

Occasionally, you will find ministers or lawyers who will be experienced in dealing with troubled marriages. See how far you can go with them. If you do not seem to go far enough, level with them and ask them to send you to someone else. It is no reflection on them, or for that matter on any professional, if you are not able to make progress with them. Just because you cannot succeed with one helper does not mean you cannot make it with others. You may not be able to find what you want on your first or even second try. If your efforts reach a dead end, it is not an indication of failure. On the contrary, it shows your interest and concern. You will be learning a great deal in going from one effort into another try. Expect dead ends as a natural part of finding the right person for you. Expecting to find the right source at the first or even second try is too much to expect. As you shop for a car, why should you not shop for the best help you can get?

Another possible source of referral could be your club or lodge. The leaders of these organizations may know more than you do in suggesting who could be of help to you. Ask them—you may not be disappointed. What do you have to lose?

Counselors

School counselors are usually able to tell you where you can find professional help or they can help you either to start a self-help group or conduct a structured program, as suggested earlier. Even though you may be embarrassed to ask them, see if you can overcome your initial embarrassment and make an appointment to see them. Although they are oriented toward helping youngsters rather than adults, they have some experience in helping people in trouble. Use them as long as they are and make themselves available.

Mental Health Personnel

Among the variety of mental health workers, you need to become aware of the immense differences in training, degrees, and background that are part of mental health teams. Among them you will find: (a) social workers, who may have a Master's degree in this specialty, that is, they have studied and received supervised experience for two additional years after college; (b) clinical psychologists, who have either a Master's degree or a Doctor of Philosophy degree, that is, they studied and were supervised in their work for four to five or more years above their Bachelor degrees; (c) psychiatrists, who have a Doctor of Medicine degree and usually have received three years of supervised experience after receiving their degree. Among psychiatrists, you may find a great variety of orientations and specializations. You may find some whose interests are close to those of other physicians and neurologists, that is, their interest lies in the physical aspects of mental illness. On the other hand, you may find psychoanalysts, that is, psychiatrists who have received additional prolonged experience above and beyond their psychiatric training.

In considering mental health personnel, you need to check on whether their professional approach is individual or marital. If they limit themselves to one person at the time and one of you is kept on the sidelines, so to speak, you do not need them. You need professional helpers who are willing to see both of you, together, at the same time, in their offices. If they insist in giving attention to one of you because he or she is "sicker" than the other, insist on being present anyway "for the experience" and because you care. Your insistence may upset them, but it may force them to see aspects of your marriage that they may not see otherwise.

In addition to these traditional mental health workers, new additions that could be of possible help to you are: (a) the mental health nurse, who may have received training in dealing with couples; (b) educational psychologists or counselors, whose interest may also lie in working with marriages (they usually receive a Doctor of Education degree after four or five years of study and supervised experience after college); (c) more and more clinics which are starting to add family life educators, who are people especially trained in dealing with sexual problems, marriage, and the family. They are especially found in family and children's services. In fact, if you have not found what you want in a mental health clinic, you may want to try family and children's services for help.

Marriage Counselors

There are experienced professionals whose specialty is troubled marriages. Among them you will find a vast range of degrees (from the A.B. to the M.A., M.S., M.Ed., Ph.D., Doctor of Theology,

Seeking Private Helpers

Ed.D., etc.), backgrounds, and levels of experience. For anyone using specifically the title "marriage counselor," check whether they are approved by the local mental health association or whether they are certified or licensed by the state in which you live. If they do not have state qualifications (certification, license, or whatever), make sure that some known professional in your community can reassure you about their qualifications. The degree in itself should not be an issue, the orientation may be relative, but their ethical competence may be something you cannot take for granted. Someone knowledgeable in your community should know about their qualifications. In case you do not know how to go about it, ask them directly to give you a name or a source where you can find additional information about them. If they cannot or refuse to do so, be extremely careful of availing yourselves of their services.

Professional Organizations

There are a large number of professional organizations in your state. If you cannot find one, you will find another. These organizations are important in safeguarding the standards of service of their members. Qualified professionals usually belong to one or more of these organizations. Check with them, or, even better, check with the state board of examiners in the capital city of your state. Ask what kind of specialties they examine and certify. There are certain professional specialties, especially in the area of marriage, that are not as yet covered by state laws. It is in states where such laws are lacking that you will find the larger number of possible quacks and charlatans. On the other hand, because there are no laws to protect you does not mean that you will not find qualified professionals. They will be members of the state organization closest to their professions.

Among the many organizations dealing with marriage and the family, those with a national or statewide membership are easily located in the capital city of your state. If you cannot find them locally, you can write to the following national organizations for qualified professionals close to you.

American Association of Marriage and Family Counselors, 225 Yale Avenue, Claremont, California, 91711. This is one of the oldest and most serious of the professional organizations. They check on the qualifications of their members and have various degrees of experience recognized by the titles their members receive in the organization. These titles range from student, to clinical member, to full member, to supervisory position. The national organization has either state or regional representatives, and its members are screened to deal with troubled marriages. Remember, however, that membership in this or other national organizations is not sufficient in and by itself to guarantee perfect fit between you two and your helper. This perfect fit does not exist.

National Alliance for Family Life, Inc., 505 Fifth Street, Huntington Beach, California, 92648. This is a relatively new but active organization that is trying to deal with all matters pertaining to marriage and the family. Of major interest to this organization is the issue of insurance. As you know, your insurance may cover mental health services for *one* of you but not for both. Insurance programs are still geared to the old view of mental health from a medical viewpoint, that an individual becomes troubled all by himself. Fortunately, there are many organizations fighting in Washington to get changes in obsolete insurance policies that discriminate against any profession except physicians. We need insurance policies that will cover marriages as well as parent-child relations and the whole family.

National Council of Family Relations, 1219 University Avenue, S.E., Minneapolis, Minnesota, 55414. Even though this is an interest group, that is, you do not need to be a professional to belong to it, this large and active organization does have a section devoted to counseling and family action. Its members can be found mostly in colleges and universities. Their national, state, or regional headquarters will be in a position to suggest names of professional helpers to you.

American Psychological Association, 1200 Seventeenth Street, N.W., Washington, D.C., 20036. This is the largest organization of psychologists in the country. However, you must remember that only a small number of these professionals are interested in working with people. In fact, many of them are more interested in working with rats (research, teaching) than with people. Even among those interested in working with people you need to check out which of them are ex-

Seeking Private Helpers

perienced in working with troubled marriages. Make sure that they list themselves as clinical psychologists.

American Psychiatric Association, 1700 Eighteenth Street, N.W., Washington, D.C., 20009. This is the largest organization of psychiatrists in this country. Both APAs in some ways determine the level of training of their members. However, in psychiatry as well as in clinical psychology, most of the training thus far has been in working with individuals. You need to check on whether the professional helper available to you has been able to get further experience in working with troubled marriages.

Another organization with a much smaller number of members is the *American Psychoanalytic Association,* composed of psychiatrists with specialized training based on the theories of Sigmund Freud. There are a variety of other organizations reflecting splinter groups from the original doctrines of Freud and his descendants. Again you need to check on the individual after you have checked on the organizations to which he belongs.

American Association of Social Workers, 1535 H Street, Suite 600, Washington, D.C., 20005. This is probably one of the largest of the mental health organizations. Among its members you may be able to find more marriage counselors than in all the previous ones combined. If you find a member of this association who is also a member of other marriage-oriented organizations, you may have found who you need.

American Association of Pastoral Counselors, 3 West 29th Street, New York, N.Y., 10001. There is more than one organization for pastoral counseling, that is, ministers who receive special training to work intensively with people. Again, your minister, priest, or rabbi will be able to check directly for you. If you do not want a religious approach, try the other organizations.

American Association of Sex Educators and Counselors, 5010 Wisconsin Avenue, Washington, D.C., 20016. Recognizing that sex and sexuality are an important part of marriage, this organization is especially concerned with sex from an educational viewpoint rather than from a viewpoint of help. Nonetheless, their programs and activities are so many that, if there is a sexual problem in your marriage, this organization could be an important source of information for you.

American Orthopsychiatric Association, 1775 Broadway, New York, N.Y., 10019. This is one of the largest mental health organizations especially interested in the welfare of children. It is composed of a variety of professional specialties and it has extended membership to teachers and other professionals with lesser credentials than was traditionally the case.

Other Organizations: There may be other organizations concerned with marriage that we may have overlooked. However, the list we have given you includes most of the serious ones to date. You should be able to contact any of them with confidence that they will try to give you the best sources of help for your marriage.

Now that you have considered self-help groups, some possible programs, made a few phone calls, written a letter or two, talked to a few professional helpers and finally succeeded in making an appointment with one, what comes next? Seeking is just the beginning. Now that you have found it, will you be able to make help work for your marriage? We will deal with this problem in the next chapter.

13
getting help

Help is where you find it and what you do with it. Whatever help you get you will need to make the most and the best of it. Only half your work is done after you have found help. Even after you get it, you will need to use it for the best advantage of your marriage.

If you cannot find the help you want in your backyard, you may need to look elsewhere for it. Get on the phone and call. If calling gets to be a chore for one of you, divide it 50-50. Each of you should be responsible for the same number of calls and each should take responsibility for looking, since both of you need to be involved in the process. If just one of you assumes this responsibility, the other one (whatever the excuses) will not be as involved and perhaps not as committed as the other. It is essential, therefore, that each of you look into different possibilities.

If and when you are settled on a choice, there are three major issues to consider: (1) time, (2) money, and (3) effort. You may have time but no money. You may have money but no time. You may have both time and money but no effort is made to involve yourselves in the very exciting process of change.

Whether you live in the country or in the city, it will take some time to go to your helper's office. Most professional helpers work daytime hours and make no exceptions as to evening or night hours. There are an increasing number of mental health facilities and a few professionals who are beginning to keep office hours in the evenings. Chances are that your first appointment will be in the daytime, so that one or both of you will have to leave work.

You may need to get a babysitter if your children are small or leave them with friends or relatives. If they want to know the reason for your going, do not be afraid to tell them. Getting help is the responsible, constructive action to take. You do not need to feel ashamed of what you are doing. On the other hand, you do not need to raise a flag, blow a trumpet, or beat a drum, letting everyone know that you are getting help. Only those in a position who need to know have to be told. Hopefully, they are sufficiently trustworthy that they will keep that information to themselves. In fact, if you are afraid that they may talk around your place of work or in the neighborhood, you may explain how you feel about this information ("I would appreciate it if you kept this information confidential").

If you really want help, you will travel as far as is needed. In fact, such travel may be an important part of working on your marriage. It is during the time you travel that you can talk with each other and perhaps reorganize your thoughts into more positive routes than you may have done thus far.

Help costs money. You are lucky if you find help in a community mental health clinic or a hospital. Use these public facilities if you can. However, you may find them crowded, with waiting lists, and with limited resources for prolonged help. Save your money, if you have any, to get private professional help, if you can get it. Make sure to look at your health insurance policy and see what it can do to help you in paying fees. More and more insurance companies and employers are recognizing the importance of marriage and the family in the emotional and mental health of their clients and employees. Almost all health insurance policies have some provision to pay part or all of mental health services. Use them all you can. Discuss fees with your helper and prepare a realistic budget that you can meet for at least three to six months. If your marriage is important to you, you will find the money.

The Difference Between Service and Help

Most people (individuals as well as institutions) provide and perform services. That is, they make themselves and their experiences

Getting Help

available to employers, clients, or customers for a salary or a fee. Lawyers, physicians, therapists, and marriage counselors sell their time and their experience to whoever needs and wants them. These people furnish services. Now, whether their services are of help to you or not is up to you! You determine if and whether the service given to you is helpful. It is impossible for helpers to make this decision for you, since they can only be responsible for providing their services in the best manner they know how.

You should understand now the difference between service and help. A professional determines the kind and level of service he provides. You are responsible for getting the service and making that service work for you. If it works for you it is helpful. If you are set in putting down all professional helpers, clearly none of them will be helpful for you. In fact, one of you may find some defect and imperfection in anyone you meet, professionally or otherwise. If you are determined to find faults and if you need perfection, then no one will be able to satisfy you. You may get the best professional in the world, but if you are set in destroying yourself and your marriage, the best qualified help will not stop you.

How Do We Know When We Have Been Helped?

You know you have been helped the day the problem that drove you to seek help no longer exists. You have been helped if each of you has changed enough to be able to keep your head up and feel good and proud of yourself. You have been helped if you sleep at night and no longer feel miserable. You have been helped if you feel like a different person from what you were before getting help. You have been helped if you feel like you are both working on a different marriage than the one you had, almost as if you are now in a second marriage. You have been helped if your neighbors and friends comment about how much better you look. You have been helped if your children behave themselves and are successful at what they are doing, especially in school. You have been helped if you both feel you can make it on your own and you realize that yourself and your marriage are the two most important things going for you in your life, well ahead of children, in-laws, job security, and money.

Shifting Gears

Each of you is now shifting gears. Up to now you may have felt that your mate, your children, or your external world needed to be changed. At this point in getting help, you may need to consider a completely different possibility—that you need to change and that changing oneself is the hardest thing in the whole world to do. Why? As we have often repeated in the course of this book, it is relatively easy to change jobs, houses, cities, and, in our society, even mates. However, no matter how many external changes we may be making, we need to contend all our lives with whatever we take along inside our skin—our self. Most of us find it so hard and painful to change ourselves that we prefer all changes to occur outside of us.

What you are going through now is perhaps the most difficult time of your life. You will find yourself angry, quick to react, short-tempered, unforgiving, sad, frustrated, etc. You and your mate are at each other's throats constantly and you use the children as scapegoats for your own unhappiness. In fact, it would not be unusual if at this time (in addition to you and your mate reacting emotionally), that your children may be "acting up" as well.

Very often it is the children's actions that awaken us to the possibility that there may be something missing in ourselves and our marriage. Whatever the children may be doing that is not paying off for them may show us what is not working in the marriage and in each of the mates.

The children may be bewildered, upset, insecure, anxious, fidgety, withdrawn, antisocial, or asocial. You need not tell them how things are going between you two, because they know. However, at this point of crisis, you need to reassure yourself in order to be able to reassure your mate and your children. The fact that your marriage is troubled does not mean that each of you will not survive. You may not survive as well, but you will, nevertheless, survive. Therefore, you need to reassure yourself that you will survive whether the marriage goes on or not. If the burden of your survival and happiness has been put on your marriage and your mate, that is too much of a burden for any relationships or any individual to bear. Your self survival depends on you, not others.

Getting Help

If you have made your mate and children responsible for your survival, you have bound yourself and them in one of the deadliest binds of all. Love under this condition becomes a commodity that is transferable according to how we behave. It is made conditional on somebody else's behavior. All of us are responsible for how we live our own lives and how we control or give up our destiny. All of us have to contend with that crazy part of ourselves that lets our better self go and attaches on others the responsibility for our behavior.

This giving up of ourself is deadly. Our mate and/or our children become bound to provide us with what we cannot give ourselves. Under these conditions, how can our self survive? Giving up responsibility for our self implies allowing others to define us as they see fit. If we define ourselves and behave in a negative, destructive fashion, we cannot ask others in constant contact with us to behave better than we do. If we define ourselves and behave in positive ways, we can make it possible for others to be at their best.

Now that help has been sought, it can be used to break the destructive patterns of the past. With help and effort on your part, you may begin to see ways of thinking and behaving that will pay off for you, your marriage, and your family.

14
making help work: getting hold of yourself

You now have started working on your marriage! You are both seeing somebody who is helping you. You are now feeling hopeful. But, there are some points you need to follow. Otherwise your time, money, and energy may be wasted. These guidelines should help you both get the most from your help. If you do not follow them, be prepared to see your efforts fail.

Assuming Personal Responsibility

If you think now that you have someone to help you, that you are no longer responsible for your marriage, you are mistaken. Your mate alone is not responsible for your marriage. *You* are also responsible. That means that instead of leaving the responsibility outside of yourself ("It's my mate's fault"), you have to start seeing what you have contributed to the troubled state of your marriage. If you think of yourself as "innocent" and of your mate as "at fault" or "guilty," start thinking otherwise. There are no guilty or innocent parties. You both are innocent and both are guilty. Each of you in your own way has contributed to the marriage going downhill. Your worrying about the negative contribution of your mate will not help. Start worrying about your own independent contribution. Instead of "you," start thinking and talking "I". Start asking yourself: "What am I contributing to this lousy situation?" "What am I doing or not doing that is making matters worse?" "What can I do to make things better for myself and my marriage?"

Making Help Work: Getting Hold of Yourself

As long as your energies are concentrated on your mate's contribution, no matter how terrible, you are wasting energy, time, and money. You may be using your mate as a way of pulling yourself up; that is, if he is a so-and-so, then you may be better than he. By putting him down, are you pulling yourself up? If this is what you are doing, watch yourself. It is a game that both can play. Your mate will start to put you down—and where does that leave you? Both of you end in the gutter, not the best place to be.

Avoiding Putting Oneself Down

You feel extremely bad, and, if you are down on those you care for, very likely you are down on yourself. When you are feeling low, it is hard to behave in winning or helpful ways. It is important at this point to make clear that just because your marriage is not working does not mean that somebody is "no good" or "bad." The major mistake in thinking this way is to think that how we behave is how we are. We are what we are, human beings who make mistakes. But because we make mistakes does not mean that we are less than human. Yet, we treat ourselves and others as if we were less than human. If we do not respect ourselves, how can we respect others?

Avoiding putting ourselves down means getting hold of ourselves and realizing that we are human and make mistakes. If we accept our human tendency to make mistakes, perhaps we can be forgiving of the mistakes of those around us. Many a marriage is wrecked by lack of forgiveness, not of others, but of ourselves.

Dealing with the Children

If the children are asking questions, consider yourself lucky. It is better for them to try to understand rather than to withdraw from the hurt around them. In fact, if they are not asking questions, they may be doing the asking by acting up in some way. Talk about how you feel and not how badly your mate is behaving. More often than not your children will need reassurance that, no matter what, they will survive and that someone will take care of them. The unknown is probably one of the most terrifying fears we have.

Looking at Yourself

Start becoming aware of the importance of your own self, your own feelings, and your own thoughts. Have you been using your mate to avoid looking at how miserable you are? Have you made your mate responsible for your happiness? Have you asked from the marriage what it cannot do? That is, to give you the happiness you cannot give yourself? Why are you so miserable? Are you trying to use your mate as a foil to avoid looking at yourself? Are you concentrating on his flaws and errors to such a degree that you have no time or energy to look at yourself?

How much of what you are doing is a repeat of the way you were raised? How much of what you are doing has to do with the way you look at your parents? With a loss you have not been able to mourn? With your inability to get in touch with your own feelings? With a past you cannot let go?

Unless each of you reads and answers these questions and many others your helper may pose for you, your marriage is not likely to improve. Marriages are for adults, and if both of you behave as parents and children to and with each other, you are doomed. Becoming an adult means assuming responsibility for one's feelings, thoughts, and actions as well as avoiding trying to read your mate's mind. If you continue talking for or about your mate, you have not passed the first step and can make no progress.

Unless each of you learns to assume responsibility for your own self, there is no hope for your marriage. Since very likely each of you gave the responsibility to the other, you need to practice over and over saying "I" or beginning your sentences with the impersonal "It."

Translating Thoughts and Feelings into Deeds

If what you think and feel is not translated into new actions, you are "spinning your wheels." If you understand yourself and you see that the way you behaved in the past did not pay off for you, then you need to consider changing. In order to obtain some change in your behavior, you need to start listening to yourself before you can listen to your mate or your helper. Listening to oneself means becoming aware of how we feel and think about any issue in our lives, starting

Making Help Work: Getting Hold of Yourself

from ourself in the cradle to seeing ourselves in the coffin. To translate your feelings and thoughts into new actions you need to practice the following ways of behavior.

Think About What You Are Going to Say

Are you going to speak again about your mate? If that is what you are planning to do, stop! Think about yourself! If what you were going to say is another accusation, a putdown, or a mind-reading statement, substitute a comment about how you feel and think about whatever issue you are facing. Avoid making threats, giving ultimatums, or expressing revengeful thoughts. Make a statement about yourself. If you cannot do it, ask your helper to assist you in practicing. If your statement is a negative one, substitute a positive one, in which you express your feelings without berating yourself or your mate.

Think About What You Have Said

After making a statement, how do you feel? If the comment you just made was a helpful one, you should feel proud about having said it. The difference between a negative and a positive statement lies in how you feel afterwards. If you have been able to express and compress what you feel in a concise, short clear sentence, you have achieved your goal. If you keep on talking, rambling on without end, you need more practice.

Listen to Your Mate and Helper

To listen does not mean to be silent or uninterested. It means to become aware of how the other one feels about any given issue in your lives. It is important for each of you to recognize your feelings and those of the other. However, you cannot recognize each other's feelings unless you start recognizing those inside of your own selves. Once you become aware of the importance of these feelings, then you will need to assert their importance. Why? Because your feelings represent you. If you are and feel important, you will want to be heard.

If, of course, you do not feel important, then your feelings will not be important either. If you do not feel important, why should anyone else think you are? If you do feel important, you will be able to recognize the importance of others, and when you listen to them, you will hear.

Think About What You Have Heard

Listening to someone, whether it is your mate or your helper, means taking it with you, considering it at least overnight, and the next day being able to form your own reaction to it. Unless you have practiced listening to yourself, you will be unable to listen to anyone else. It is important, therefore, for both of you to practice, to avoid wasting time. Use your helper to help you on this crucial matter.

Dropping the Past

The past is important and there is a great deal to be learned from your past life about your mistakes. However, if you are using the past as a sword or an axe over your mate's head, you may as well give up. Bringing up the unpleasant past with your mate is the best way of getting lost in it and will teach nothing. Let your helper assist you to learn from your own past but avoid using it to beat your mate. Using the past like a weapon is another way of avoiding responsibility for oneself by putting the responsibility on your mate. We would say that dwelling on the past may well be one of the best ways to break up a marriage.

Dropping the Future

Dropping the future does not mean not making plans or considering what to do in the future. It means not to mortgage the present for the future. I know of many couples that saved money, sacrificed, and worked for the future. In the meantime, they were making themselves miserable in the present. However, if the present is sacrificed for the future, you are both losing perspective on where you are. Planning for the future is important, but forgetting the present for the future is dangerous.

Living in the Present

If you two cannot enjoy each other *now,* when will you? If you two cannot live enjoyably in the present, how can you possibly hope to live enjoyably in the future? Living in the present does not mean that you have to forget about tomorrow or that you mortgage the future to live today. Not at all. It means living each day to the fullest without the dread of the past or fear of the future. If you do not understand this, discuss this matter further with your helper. Living in the present means to be able to take each day as it comes, after you have planned for it. It does not mean to be helpless victims of life as it occurs, but means being in charge of your lives to the point of being able to enjoy them.

Separating Feelings from Actions

Many of us are unable to separate how we feel from how we act. In fact, many of us think that these two processes are one and the same. This is a very destructive pitfall. Feelings and doings are two completely distinct, separate processes. We may feel sad, hurt, and desperate. However, we have a wide range of choices of action about what to do concerning these feelings, especially doing nothing, but frankly acknowledging them to ourselves and to our mate. Listen to your feelings, avoid doing anything about them, except sharing them with your mate and your helper.

15
the tasks of marriage enhancement

We have found it useful to practice seven different points in our own marriage and in our practice of marriage counseling. We would like to share these points with you to use in your own situations.

Seeing the Good

Every human problem has at least two sides, the positive and the negative. You can dwell, for instance, on the negatives of your present situation and do nothing positive so that they will remain what they appear, negatives. On the other hand, you can look at the present crisis as a way of forcing change upon you and your marriage and your life. If the change is for the better, and you learn something from this experience, then you can advance on to a higher level in your marriage. We recently saw a couple in their middle thirties who were wrestling and wrenching in the throes of finding themselves and each other. The husband felt that the last five years, since he had married, were the worst of his life. They will be, if he learns nothing from them. However, if the present turmoil and seeking help give him a chance to learn more about himself as a man, husband, and father, then perhaps he needed those five "bad" years to find himself.

Seeing the good also means dwelling on the positive aspects of those near you. No matter how negative your feelings may be at present, your mate must have many positive qualities or you would not have chosen him in the first place. Think back to your courtship, since, after all, your choice of mate reflects on you. You can hardly think well of yourself if you do not think well of your mate. Thinking negatively about your mate is too costly to your own self-respect. The rewards of seeing positives are greater than the costs of seeing negatives in oneself and others.

Caring

Doing our chores every day and seeing to it that they are done well is caring. Going to work, getting the job done, assuming the daily routine, and seeing that the humdrum drudgery of everyday details are taken care of is caring. Caring, however, means more. It means feeling that one is important. If you care for yourself, it means that you are aware of the importance of your uniqueness. There is no one like you! If you are important, you need to take care of yourself. We also take care of those who are important to us. That is what marriage and the family is all about. However, you cannot take good care of others unless you can and do take good care of yourself first. If you respect yourself, you will expect others to respect you and you will be able to respect them. If you respect yourself, your mate and children will respect you, too. If you do not, neither will they.

Caring works best under mutual or reciprocal circumstances. If you want your relationships to be two-way streets, make sure you keep the traffic going both ways! If the traffic is mostly in one direction, someone is cheating himself!

Sharing Hurt Feelings

Anyone will share our victories and celebrations, even strangers, but who will share our defeats, our hurts, and our pain? Most of us do not know how to handle our feelings of grief, sorrow, abandonment, fear, and loneliness. Why? Because no one taught us properly. It is useless to go back and find out how our parents did it. They did it the best they knew how. How can we learn how to share those feelings? Would you believe that a great deal of our problems come from our inability to share these feelings of hurt? The next time you feel angry or indignant, ask yourself: How much of this feeling is hurt? If your answer is "A great deal," you may start to consider sharing some if not all of these feelings with your mate. In this area, women have it easier than men. They have been trained to express their feelings much better than men.

Sharing the inevitable pain that life brings us is one of the main tasks of marriage. Sharing pain is the true intimacy of marriage, for we can truly share and feel the pain of only those we deeply care for. When they hurt, we hurt.

Forgiveness

Forgiving and forgetting is one of the most difficult things to do in marriage. Bringing up past wrongs can be deadly to a marriage. How often do you find yourselves bringing up small, petty, sometimes imaginary slights and hurts? Have you found it helpful to bring up the past to hit each other with it? If you have, continue; if you have not, consider the following.

1) There is nothing you can do the change the past. However, there is an awful lot you can do to change yourself in the present.

2) Spending any time talking about the past takes away from considering the present. The present is important. The past is gone.

3) If the past points out what mistakes you have made, use it to correct them.

4) If you are using past occurrences to berate your mate, to show him what a so-and-so he is, you are the one who is jeopardizing the marriage more than anyone else.

5) Whatever your mate has done in the past to burden your marriage, you have burdened it in other ways that you are avoiding looking at because your energy is being invested in what your mate has done rather than finding out what you have done.

6) Just because either one of you behaved like a so-and-so in the past does not mean you cannot behave better in the present.

7) Bringing up the past belittles you. Considering the present and the future enhances you.

8) If you cannot forgive your human weaknesses and mistakes, you will not be able to forgive others, especially your mate. This lack of forgiveness will produce a continuous tug-of-war—a form of behavior that sends millions of marriages to the divorce courts.

Forgiveness means understanding the frailty of our human existence. It means knowing that just because we make a mistake does not mean we are "all bad." It means that we need to forgive ourselves before we can forgive others. It means cancelling the demand for perfection we make of ourselves and of those we love.

Responsibility

Each of us is responsible for his or her own happiness. Letting someone take this awesome responsibility from us means giving up of one's self. In addition to taking the responsibility for our actions, we need to make sure that we are in charge of and in control of ourselves. This is what is meant by "to thine own self be true." Giving up this responsibility is the beginning of hell on earth, since no one else can be responsible for how we live our lives except ourselves.

We have seen countless couples who have claimed that their first and only thought was to make the other mate happy. Yet with all these claims and counterclaims, both found themselves extremely unhappy. These couples had fallen into the trap of believing a supposedly romantic and religious ideal that involves giving up one's self for the other's happiness; even though one of the major rules ever given relates to loving our neighbor as ourself. Ourself is the closest neighbor we have. If we cannot take care of this self, how can we take care of our neighbor? We often think that selfhood means selfishness and cannot tell the difference between the two.

Protectiveness

To protect ourselves we need to be continually vigilant. We are under continuous attack to give up and give in to external pressures. If we protect ourselves, we can then protect our marriage. If we protect our marriage, we can then protect our children.

We must protect these three—ourselves, our marriage, and our children—in that order. If your priorities get mixed up to the point that you think the children come before you or your marriage, ask yourself this question: What will happen to you and your marriage after the children are grown and gone? If you do not protect it now, how will the marriage work then? After the children have left and you two are alone, one of you will die before the other. Then who will take care of your self, especially if you have given up your self for your marriage or your children?

Think about other priorities, such as work. If work has become so important that your marriage is second to it, beware. Work can be a dangerous priority and even worse than putting children first. Especially when you use your work to define yourself. Ask yourself: How many jobs do I want or can I have? How many marriages and families do I want or can I have? Answer by thinking how many you can have of each and then see if you can look at your job with a different perspective. How many executives have climbed the ladder of success leaving their marriages behind, only to find once at the top that that kind of success means nothing if it cannot be shared? Furthermore, how about retirement? If you define yourself by your job, what will happen to you and your marriage once you retire? If you have invested little energy in your marriage, do not expect it to pay dividends to you. Marriage is like savings: the more you invest in it, the more you get back. However, if what you put in is phoney and not truly representative of your own self, do not expect to get a real marriage. You will get a phoney marriage!

Enjoyment

Enjoyment and pleasure in life and marriage derive from our feeling good about ourselves. How do we feel good? By behaving in ways that pay off for ourselves and those we love. It means behaving in prideful ways. Once this feeling of accomplishment is achieved, then pleasure and enjoyment can be had in the kitchen, in the bedroom, in the living room. That is where the action is.

16
when help seems to fail

You have gone for professional help and apparently it did not take. Whatever was supposed to work did not. You both feel angry, frustrated, and extremely sad and upset. Your hopes and expectations were not fulfilled. Now you are looking at the shambles of your life and of your marriage. You and your mate have not been able to use the help given to decide whether to live together happily or separate happily. Many couples have an investment in living miserably together or separately. What is your hidden reason? How did you make the help fail?

Why Did Help Fail?

To learn something from your experience you need to look at all of the possibilities for your inability to get what you needed. If you can learn from your failures, you are a success. If you learn nothing from your successes, you may turn into a failure.

Your Contribution

Stop wondering whose fault it was. Fault is assigned when people do not want to take responsibility for their own selves. Where did you stray? What did you do that made it impossible for the helper to help you? Did you expect too much from him? Did you expect too little? Did you level with him or her?

By now you may feel as if all of your resources, both inside and outside of your marriage, have been used. You may feel empty, used, tired, unhappy, miserable. You feel that the situation is hopeless and worse than it was before you started. In fact, you may wish you had never started and left well enough alone.

Let us ask a few questions at this point to see how bad things really are:

1) Are you still married to each other? If the answer is yes, it means that you have a strong marriage. It may not be the kind of marriage you want, but apparently it withstood the pressures of trying to change.

2) Did you work together on trying to change? Maybe at this point you see no immediate returns and no change. However, is not the fact that you shared working together, even if apparently unsuccessfully, enough of a positive sign for you? How many positive signs do you need?

3) Is where you are today different from where you were yesterday? Perhaps what you have learned in the process of change is that your marriage is even in worse shape than you thought it was to begin with. By the same token, you may have learned that your marriage is in better shape than you thought it was.

4) No matter how disappointed and tired you may feel, see if you can find some positives in yourself and your marriage. For instance, how about your awareness? Are you more aware than you were before? How about your attitude? Has your attitude changed? How about your feelings? Do you feel better about yourself? How about your thinking? Do you think differently about yourself and your marriage than you did before? How about your acting? Do you act in more positive ways than you did before you got help?

If all of these areas have not changed, it means that you have not really made use of your help. It may mean that deep down you have left all the responsibility for your marriage to your mate or your helper rather than taking your part of it.

How Can You Turn a Failure into a Success?

Only by not giving up the fight and trying to get the best for yourself and your marriage can you turn failure into success.

Of course, both success and failure may be relative words. If you have learned something new about yourself and your marriage, then

When Help Seems to Fail

your past step was not a failure. Perhaps you expected drastic changes that did not take place. Then be thankful for a few changes that may not make your life enjoyable as yet but at least livable. Perhaps this try may have helped you see how unsuited you are for each other. Are you ready to split? If you are not, then you are ready for some of the alternatives outlined and described here.

Trying Again—Exploring Other Choices

Go back, retrace your steps, and find out whether what previously seemed to be a blind alley is still a dead end street. What may have appeared as such then may offer a brand new opportunity for both of you. If you still care for each other, keep on asking for help and getting it. By now you may be ready to throw in the towel and give up. Great! Maybe you both need to reach rock bottom before you can start again. We did say earlier that things may get worse before they get better. Perhaps you are now experiencing what we were talking about then.

The issue is not whether you have failed and reached rock bottom; the issue is whether you both can pull yourselves up and try again. If you do not give up and are strong enough to ask for help again, you may have won part of the battle.

There are no magic numbers about how many times you need to try. One source states seventy times seven. Does it mean that because you are not making it that you both are no good and that you are not suited for each other? Consider the possibility that you both may be so tough and powerful that neither one of you is able and willing to give up. Have you tried giving up instead of giving in? Try it. It may work wonders for you.

Actually, to be perfectly honest, even if the help you sought worked for both of you, you would have nothing to lose by trying out other possibilities. You are both entitled to as many choices this country of ours offers you. By all means, take them.

Do You Want Your Marriage?

As you are now hurting from what you see as a failure, you can use this time of hurt, pain, and depression to ask yourself the crucial question: "Do you want to stay married to each other?" If you do, why? Do you want to stay married to each other out of weakness you see in yourself and in your mate? Do you stay married to each other out of fear? Because you can not do better than what you have already? Do you want to stay married because you are afraid of change, whether for the better or for the worse?

What could you do if you were not married to each other? Could you explore other possibilities, get to know other people? Could you do alone what you could not do married? Exactly what?

Do You Want a Divorce?

If you do not want to stay married to each other, is divorce the only alternative? What would each of you gain from a divorce? More money? More friends? Greater freedom? Less hassle? Greater self-respect? Ask yourself these questions and answer them in terms of whether you cannot get the same goals in your marriage. If you have not received what you wanted in your marriage, how did you let yourself down? Never mind your mate. How did you fail in not getting what you wanted out of your marriage? Answer that question as honestly as you can, then see whether you can approach your marriage from a different perspective than you had before. Above all, make sure of being honest with yourself, because the only one being fooled is you and nobody else.

Have you been honest with yourself? If you can answer yes, then you may need help for yourself alone, because the marriage cannot do more for you now. Other choices may be other groups, taking your children along for family therapy, living with your close relatives (parents, brothers and sisters), separating for a while, or tabling any decision for a definite time.

Conclusion

We want to conclude with a story about a couple both of us had been seeing for quite some time for more sessions than we care to mention. Even though they had many, many assets and resources, they continued their bickering, putdowns, fighting, and disagreements. We used all of the resources we had available to us. We saw them together, we saw them separately, we switched as individual therapists from one to another. We saw them with their children. We had them involved in many different enrichment programs. We confessed our helplessness in helping them and acknowledged repeatedly our sense of defeat and failure. Finally, we did not specify an appointment because they were going on vacation and their schedule was not clear. However, they did call to let us know we would hear from them as soon as they came back from vacation. After we did not hear from them for three weeks we called to see what was happening. To our inquiry on the phone, the wife quite cheerfully informed us they were getting along much better and that they would come to see us for a final appointment but that they "had decided to build themselves up instead of tearing each other down." When this decision had been made, things had started to get better for both of them. Clearly a decision had been made and that decision is ours and ours alone. In this book, we have tried to suggest that there is a whole range of choices between a troubled marriage or no marriage: We can all have a better marriage, if we want to!